50 Canadian Cake Recipes for Home

By: Kelly Johnson

Table of Contents

- Nanaimo Bars Cake
- Maple Syrup Cake
- Butter Tart Cake
- Blueberry Grunt Cake
- Pouding Chômeur Cake
- Saskatoon Berry Cake
- Beaver Tail Cake
- Timbit Cake
- Canadian Carrot Cake
- Montreal Bagel Cake
- Prince Edward Island Potato Cake
- Niagara Peach Cake
- Alberta Wild Rose Cake
- Manitoba Morden Blush Cake
- British Columbia Apple Cake
- Canadian Butter Cake
- Butter Tart Bundt Cake
- Hudson's Bay Company Cake
- Canadian Maple Walnut Cake
- Quebec Sugar Pie Cake
- Toronto Blueberry Cheesecake Cake
- Nova Scotia Blueberry Grunt Cake
- Newfoundland Jam Jam Cake
- Yukon Gold Rush Cake
- Banff Rocky Road Cake
- Vancouver Island Blackberry Cake
- Ottawa Beaver Tail Cake
- Quebec Maple Buttercream Cake
- Calgary Stampede Cake
- Ontario Black Forest Cake
- British Columbia Rainforest Cake
- Quebec Maple Pecan Cake
- Alberta Honey Cake
- Saskatchewan Saskatoon Berry Cake
- PEI Raspberry Cake

- Montreal Smoked Meat Cake
- Toronto Butter Tart Cake
- Vancouver Coffee Crisp Cake
- Ottawa Maple Bacon Cake
- Niagara Peach Melba Cake
- Manitoba Tiger Tail Cake
- Quebec Tourtière Cake
- Alberta Beef Cake
- Saskatchewan Wheat Cake
- Vancouver Salmon Cake
- Calgary Beef-on-Bun Cake
- Ontario Garlic Cake
- British Columbia Smoked Salmon Cake
- Newfoundland Pea Soup Cake
- Yukon Sourdough Cake

Nanaimo Bars Cake

Ingredients:

For the Cake Layers:

- 2 cups graham cracker crumbs
- 1 cup shredded coconut
- 1/2 cup chopped walnuts or pecans
- 1/2 cup cocoa powder
- 1/2 cup granulated sugar
- 1 cup unsalted butter, melted
- 2 large eggs, beaten

For the Filling:

- 1/2 cup unsalted butter, softened
- 2 cups powdered sugar (icing sugar)
- 2 tablespoons vanilla custard powder or instant vanilla pudding mix
- 3-4 tablespoons milk or cream

For the Chocolate Ganache:

- 1 cup semi-sweet or dark chocolate chips
- 1/2 cup heavy cream
- 1 tablespoon unsalted butter

Instructions:

1. **Prepare the Cake Layers:**
    - In a large bowl, combine graham cracker crumbs, shredded coconut, chopped nuts, cocoa powder, and granulated sugar.
    - Add melted butter and beaten eggs, mixing until well combined.
    - Press the mixture firmly into the bottom of two greased and parchment-lined 9-inch round cake pans.
    - Bake at 350°F (175°C) for about 10-12 minutes until set. Let cool completely.
2. **Make the Filling:**
    - In a mixing bowl, cream together softened butter, powdered sugar, and vanilla custard powder (or instant vanilla pudding mix).
    - Gradually add milk or cream, mixing until smooth and spreadable. Adjust consistency as needed with more milk or powdered sugar.
3. **Assemble the Cake:**
    - Place one cooled cake layer on a serving plate.
    - Spread a generous layer of the filling evenly over the cake layer.
    - Place the second cake layer on top and gently press down.
4. **Prepare the Chocolate Ganache:**
    - In a small saucepan, heat heavy cream until just simmering (do not boil).
    - Remove from heat and pour over chocolate chips in a heatproof bowl. Let sit for 1-2 minutes.

        - Stir gently until smooth and glossy, then stir in butter until melted and fully incorporated.
5. **Finish the Cake:**
        - Pour the chocolate ganache over the top of the cake, allowing it to drip down the sides.
        - Refrigerate the cake for at least 1-2 hours to set the ganache and filling before serving.
6. **Serve and Enjoy:**
        - Slice and serve chilled, enjoying the rich layers reminiscent of the classic Nanaimo bars in cake form!

This Nanaimo Bars Cake combines the beloved flavors of chocolate, coconut, and creamy filling in a new and delightful presentation. It's perfect for special occasions or anytime you crave a taste of Canadian dessert tradition!

Maple Syrup Cake

Ingredients:

- 1 cup (240 ml) maple syrup
- 3/4 cup (170 g) unsalted butter, softened
- 3/4 cup (150 g) granulated sugar
- 3 large eggs
- 1 tsp vanilla extract
- 2 1/2 cups (300 g) all-purpose flour
- 2 tsp baking powder
- 1/2 tsp baking soda
- 1/2 tsp salt
- 1 cup (240 ml) buttermilk

Instructions:

1. **Preheat** your oven to 350°F (175°C). Grease and flour a 9-inch (23 cm) round cake pan or line it with parchment paper.
2. **Cream** together the softened butter and sugar in a mixing bowl until light and fluffy.
3. **Add** the eggs one at a time, beating well after each addition. Stir in the vanilla extract.
4. **In another bowl**, whisk together the flour, baking powder, baking soda, and salt.
5. **Gradually add** the dry ingredients to the butter mixture, alternating with the buttermilk, beginning and ending with the dry ingredients. Mix until just combined.
6. **Pour** the batter into the prepared cake pan and smooth the top with a spatula.
7. **Bake** in the preheated oven for 30-35 minutes, or until a toothpick inserted into the center comes out clean.
8. **Cool** the cake in the pan for 10 minutes, then turn it out onto a wire rack to cool completely.

Maple Syrup Frosting (optional):

- 1/2 cup (120 ml) maple syrup
- 1/2 cup (115 g) unsalted butter, softened
- 2 cups (240 g) powdered sugar
- 1 tsp vanilla extract
- Pinch of salt

1. **Beat** the softened butter until smooth and creamy.
2. **Gradually add** the powdered sugar, maple syrup, vanilla extract, and salt, beating until smooth and fluffy.
3. **Spread** or **pipe** the frosting over the cooled cake. Optionally, drizzle with additional maple syrup for extra flavor.

Enjoy your homemade Maple Syrup Cake! Adjust the sweetness or maple intensity to your liking by varying the amount of maple syrup in both the cake and frosting.

Butter Tart Cake

Ingredients:

For the Cake:

- 1 cup (240 ml) unsalted butter, softened
- 1 cup (200 g) granulated sugar
- 3 large eggs
- 1 tsp vanilla extract
- 1 1/2 cups (180 g) all-purpose flour
- 1 1/2 tsp baking powder
- 1/2 tsp salt
- 1/2 cup (120 ml) milk

For the Butter Tart Filling:

- 1/2 cup (120 ml) maple syrup
- 1/2 cup (100 g) packed brown sugar
- 1/4 cup (60 ml) melted butter
- 1 large egg
- 1 tsp vanilla extract
- 1/2 cup (60 g) chopped pecans (optional)

Instructions:

1. **Preheat** your oven to 350°F (175°C). Grease and flour a 9-inch (23 cm) round cake pan or line it with parchment paper.
2. **Make the Butter Tart Filling:**
   - In a bowl, whisk together the maple syrup, brown sugar, melted butter, egg, and vanilla extract until smooth. Stir in the chopped pecans if using.
3. **Prepare the Cake Batter:**
   - In a separate mixing bowl, cream together the softened butter and granulated sugar until light and fluffy.
   - Beat in the eggs, one at a time, until well combined. Stir in the vanilla extract.
4. **Combine Dry Ingredients:**
   - In another bowl, whisk together the flour, baking powder, and salt.
5. **Mix the Batter:**
   - Gradually add the dry ingredients to the butter mixture, alternating with the milk, beginning and ending with the dry ingredients. Mix until just combined.
6. **Assemble the Cake:**
   - Spread half of the cake batter into the prepared cake pan.
   - Pour the Butter Tart Filling evenly over the batter in the pan.
   - Carefully spoon the remaining cake batter over the filling, spreading it evenly to cover.
7. **Bake:**
   - Bake in the preheated oven for 35-40 minutes, or until a toothpick inserted into the center comes out clean.
8. **Cool and Serve:**

- Allow the cake to cool in the pan for 10 minutes, then transfer it to a wire rack to cool completely.
9. **Optional Glaze:**
    - You can drizzle the cooled cake with a simple glaze made from powdered sugar and a little milk for extra sweetness, if desired.

Enjoy your Butter Tart Cake, a wonderful fusion of cake and the beloved flavors of Canadian butter tarts!

Blueberry Grunt Cake

Ingredients:

For the Cake:

- 1/2 cup (115 g) unsalted butter, softened
- 1 cup (200 g) granulated sugar
- 2 large eggs
- 1 tsp vanilla extract
- 2 cups (250 g) all-purpose flour
- 2 tsp baking powder
- 1/2 tsp salt
- 1/2 cup (120 ml) milk

For the Blueberry Grunt Topping:

- 4 cups (500 g) fresh or frozen blueberries
- 1/2 cup (100 g) granulated sugar
- 1 tbsp lemon juice
- 1/2 tsp cinnamon
- 1/4 cup (60 ml) water

Instructions:

1. **Preheat** your oven to 350°F (175°C). Grease and flour a 9x13-inch (23x33 cm) baking dish or line it with parchment paper.
2. **Prepare the Blueberry Grunt Topping:**
    - In a saucepan, combine the blueberries, sugar, lemon juice, cinnamon, and water.
    - Bring to a simmer over medium heat, stirring occasionally. Cook for about 5-7 minutes until the blueberries are juicy and slightly thickened. Remove from heat and set aside.
3. **Make the Cake Batter:**
    - In a large mixing bowl, cream together the softened butter and sugar until light and fluffy.
    - Beat in the eggs, one at a time, until well combined. Stir in the vanilla extract.
4. **Combine Dry Ingredients:**
    - In another bowl, whisk together the flour, baking powder, and salt.
5. **Mix the Batter:**
    - Gradually add the dry ingredients to the butter mixture, alternating with the milk, beginning and ending with the dry ingredients. Mix until just combined.
6. **Assemble the Cake:**
    - Spread the cake batter evenly into the prepared baking dish.
7. **Add the Blueberry Grunt Topping:**
    - Spoon the prepared blueberry mixture evenly over the cake batter.
8. **Bake:**
    - Bake in the preheated oven for 35-40 minutes, or until a toothpick inserted into the center of the cake comes out clean.
9. **Serve:**

- Allow the cake to cool slightly before serving. Serve warm or at room temperature, optionally with a scoop of vanilla ice cream or a dollop of whipped cream.

Enjoy your delicious Blueberry Grunt Cake, perfect for showcasing the sweetness of blueberries in a delightful cake form!

Pouding Chômeur Cake

Ingredients:

For the Cake:

- 1/2 cup (115 g) unsalted butter, softened
- 1 cup (200 g) granulated sugar
- 2 large eggs
- 1 tsp vanilla extract
- 1 1/2 cups (180 g) all-purpose flour
- 2 tsp baking powder
- 1/2 tsp salt
- 3/4 cup (180 ml) milk

For the Sauce:

- 1 cup (200 g) packed brown sugar
- 1 cup (240 ml) water
- 1/4 cup (60 ml) maple syrup or golden syrup
- 1/4 cup (60 ml) heavy cream
- 1/4 cup (60 g) unsalted butter

Instructions:

1. **Preheat** your oven to 350°F (175°C). Grease a 9x9-inch (23x23 cm) square baking dish or a similar-sized baking pan.
2. **Make the Cake Batter:**
    - In a large mixing bowl, cream together the softened butter and granulated sugar until light and fluffy.
    - Beat in the eggs, one at a time, until well combined. Stir in the vanilla extract.
3. **Combine Dry Ingredients:**
    - In another bowl, whisk together the flour, baking powder, and salt.
4. **Mix the Batter:**
    - Gradually add the dry ingredients to the butter mixture, alternating with the milk, beginning and ending with the dry ingredients. Mix until just combined.
5. **Prepare the Sauce:**
    - In a saucepan, combine the brown sugar, water, maple syrup (or golden syrup), heavy cream, and butter. Bring to a boil over medium-high heat, stirring constantly. Reduce the heat and simmer for 5 minutes, stirring occasionally. Remove from heat and set aside.
6. **Assemble the Cake:**
    - Pour the cake batter into the prepared baking dish, spreading it evenly.
7. **Add the Sauce:**
    - Carefully pour the prepared sauce over the cake batter. Do not stir.
8. **Bake:**
    - Bake in the preheated oven for 30-35 minutes, or until the cake is golden brown and a toothpick inserted into the center comes out clean.
9. **Serve:**

- Serve the Pouding Chômeur Cake warm. It can be enjoyed on its own or with a scoop of vanilla ice cream or whipped cream.

This dessert is perfect for those who enjoy sweet and comforting treats, with a lovely balance of cake and a rich, syrupy sauce. Enjoy your homemade Pouding Chômeur Cake!

Saskatoon Berry Cake

Ingredients:

For the Cake:

- 1/2 cup (115 g) unsalted butter, softened
- 1 cup (200 g) granulated sugar
- 2 large eggs
- 1 tsp vanilla extract
- 1 1/2 cups (180 g) all-purpose flour
- 2 tsp baking powder
- 1/2 tsp salt
- 1/2 cup (120 ml) milk

For the Saskatoon Berry Filling:

- 3 cups (400 g) fresh Saskatoon berries, rinsed and drained (or frozen, thawed and drained)
- 1/4 cup (50 g) granulated sugar
- 1 tbsp lemon juice
- 1 tbsp cornstarch

Optional Streusel Topping:

- 1/4 cup (50 g) granulated sugar
- 1/4 cup (30 g) all-purpose flour
- 2 tbsp unsalted butter, cold and cut into small pieces

Instructions:

1. **Preheat** your oven to 350°F (175°C). Grease and flour a 9-inch (23 cm) round cake pan or line it with parchment paper.
2. **Make the Saskatoon Berry Filling:**
    - In a medium bowl, gently toss together the Saskatoon berries, granulated sugar, lemon juice, and cornstarch until the berries are coated. Set aside.
3. **Make the Cake Batter:**
    - In a large mixing bowl, cream together the softened butter and granulated sugar until light and fluffy.
    - Beat in the eggs, one at a time, until well combined. Stir in the vanilla extract.
4. **Combine Dry Ingredients:**
    - In another bowl, whisk together the flour, baking powder, and salt.
5. **Mix the Batter:**
    - Gradually add the dry ingredients to the butter mixture, alternating with the milk, beginning and ending with the dry ingredients. Mix until just combined.
6. **Assemble the Cake:**
    - Spread half of the cake batter into the prepared cake pan.
    - Spoon the Saskatoon berry filling evenly over the batter.
    - Carefully spoon the remaining cake batter over the filling, spreading it evenly to cover.

7. **Optional Streusel Topping:**
   - In a small bowl, combine the granulated sugar and flour. Cut in the cold butter pieces using a pastry cutter or your fingers until the mixture resembles coarse crumbs. Sprinkle evenly over the cake batter.
8. **Bake:**
   - Bake in the preheated oven for 45-50 minutes, or until a toothpick inserted into the center comes out clean and the cake is golden brown.
9. **Cool and Serve:**
   - Allow the cake to cool in the pan for 10 minutes, then transfer it to a wire rack to cool completely.
10. **Serve:**
- Serve the Saskatoon Berry Cake warm or at room temperature. Optionally, serve with a dollop of whipped cream or vanilla ice cream.

Enjoy your Saskatoon Berry Cake, a wonderful dessert that showcases the delicious flavor of Saskatoon berries!

Beaver Tail Cake

Ingredients:

For the Cake:

- 1 cup (240 ml) milk
- 1 tbsp vinegar
- 1 3/4 cups (220 g) all-purpose flour
- 1 tsp baking powder
- 1/2 tsp baking soda
- 1/4 tsp salt
- 1/2 cup (115 g) unsalted butter, softened
- 1 cup (200 g) granulated sugar
- 2 large eggs
- 1 tsp vanilla extract

For the Topping:

- 1/4 cup (60 g) unsalted butter, melted
- 1/2 cup (100 g) granulated sugar
- 1 tbsp ground cinnamon

Optional Glaze:

- 1 cup (120 g) powdered sugar
- 2-3 tbsp milk or water
- 1/2 tsp vanilla extract

Instructions:

1. **Preheat** your oven to 350°F (175°C). Grease and flour a 9x13-inch (23x33 cm) baking dish or line it with parchment paper.
2. **Prepare the Cake Batter:**
    - In a small bowl or measuring cup, combine the milk and vinegar. Stir and let sit for 5-10 minutes to sour the milk (this creates a buttermilk substitute).
    - In a medium bowl, whisk together the flour, baking powder, baking soda, and salt.
3. **Cream the Butter and Sugar:**
    - In a large mixing bowl, cream together the softened butter and granulated sugar until light and fluffy.
4. **Add Eggs and Vanilla:**
    - Beat in the eggs, one at a time, until well combined. Stir in the vanilla extract.
5. **Combine Wet and Dry Ingredients:**
    - Gradually add the flour mixture to the butter mixture, alternating with the soured milk, beginning and ending with the flour mixture. Mix until just combined.
6. **Bake the Cake:**
    - Spread the cake batter evenly into the prepared baking dish.

- Bake in the preheated oven for 25-30 minutes, or until a toothpick inserted into the center comes out clean.
7. **Prepare the Topping:**
    - While the cake is baking, melt the butter in a small bowl. In another small bowl, mix together the granulated sugar and ground cinnamon.
8. **Assemble the Cake:**
    - As soon as the cake is done baking and while it's still hot, brush the melted butter evenly over the top of the cake.
    - Sprinkle the cinnamon sugar mixture evenly over the buttered cake.
9. **Optional Glaze:**
    - In a small bowl, whisk together the powdered sugar, milk or water, and vanilla extract until smooth. Drizzle the glaze over the cooled cake.
10. **Serve:**
    - Allow the cake to cool slightly before serving. Serve warm or at room temperature.

Enjoy your homemade BeaverTail Cake, reminiscent of the beloved Canadian pastry, with its delicious cinnamon sugar topping and optional sweet glaze!

Timbit Cake

Ingredients:

For the Cake:

- 1 3/4 cups (220 g) all-purpose flour
- 1 1/2 tsp baking powder
- 1/2 tsp baking soda
- 1/4 tsp salt
- 1/2 cup (115 g) unsalted butter, softened
- 3/4 cup (150 g) granulated sugar
- 2 large eggs
- 1 tsp vanilla extract
- 1 cup (240 ml) buttermilk

For the Glaze:

- 1 cup (120 g) powdered sugar
- 2-3 tbsp milk or water
- 1/2 tsp vanilla extract

For Decorating (Optional):

- Assorted Timbits (doughnut holes)

Instructions:

1. **Preheat** your oven to 350°F (175°C). Grease and flour a 9-inch (23 cm) round cake pan or line it with parchment paper.
2. **Prepare the Cake Batter:**
    - In a medium bowl, whisk together the flour, baking powder, baking soda, and salt.
3. **Cream the Butter and Sugar:**
    - In a large mixing bowl, cream together the softened butter and granulated sugar until light and fluffy.
4. **Add Eggs and Vanilla:**
    - Beat in the eggs, one at a time, until well combined. Stir in the vanilla extract.
5. **Combine Wet and Dry Ingredients:**
    - Gradually add the flour mixture to the butter mixture, alternating with the buttermilk, beginning and ending with the flour mixture. Mix until just combined.
6. **Bake the Cake:**
    - Spread the cake batter evenly into the prepared cake pan.
    - Bake in the preheated oven for 25-30 minutes, or until a toothpick inserted into the center comes out clean.
7. **Cool the Cake:**
    - Allow the cake to cool in the pan for 10 minutes, then transfer it to a wire rack to cool completely.
8. **Prepare the Glaze:**

- In a small bowl, whisk together the powdered sugar, milk or water, and vanilla extract until smooth. Adjust the consistency by adding more milk or powdered sugar as needed.
9. **Glaze the Cake:**
    - Once the cake is completely cooled, drizzle the glaze evenly over the top of the cake.
10. **Decorate (Optional):**
    - If desired, decorate the top of the cake with assorted Timbits (doughnut holes) for a fun and festive look.
11. **Serve:**
    - Slice and serve your Timbit Cake, enjoying the playful essence of Timbits in cake form!

This Timbit Cake is sure to delight with its tender crumb and sweet glaze, capturing the essence of everyone's favorite Canadian doughnut holes.

Canadian Carrot Cake

Ingredients:

- 2 cups all-purpose flour
- 2 teaspoons baking powder
- 1 1/2 teaspoons baking soda
- 1/2 teaspoon salt
- 2 teaspoons ground cinnamon
- 1/2 teaspoon ground nutmeg
- 4 large eggs
- 1 1/2 cups granulated sugar
- 1 cup vegetable oil
- 2 cups grated carrots (about 4-5 medium carrots)
- 1 cup chopped walnuts or pecans (optional)
- 1 teaspoon vanilla extract

Cream Cheese Frosting:

- 8 oz (225g) cream cheese, softened
- 1/2 cup (115g) unsalted butter, softened
- 4 cups powdered sugar
- 1 teaspoon vanilla extract

Instructions:

1. Preheat your oven to 350°F (175°C). Grease and flour two 9-inch round cake pans or line them with parchment paper.
2. In a large bowl, whisk together flour, baking powder, baking soda, salt, cinnamon, and nutmeg.
3. In another bowl, beat eggs and sugar until well combined and slightly thickened. Gradually beat in oil until well blended. Stir in grated carrots, nuts (if using), and vanilla extract.
4. Gradually add the dry ingredients to the wet ingredients, stirring until just combined.
5. Divide the batter evenly between the prepared cake pans.
6. Bake for 25-30 minutes, or until a toothpick inserted into the center of the cakes comes out clean.
7. Remove from the oven and let the cakes cool in the pans for 10 minutes. Then, transfer them to wire racks to cool completely.

For the Cream Cheese Frosting:

1. In a large bowl, beat cream cheese and butter until smooth and creamy.
2. Gradually add powdered sugar, one cup at a time, beating well after each addition.
3. Beat in vanilla extract until smooth and creamy.
4. Once the cakes are completely cooled, frost the top of one cake layer with about 1/3 of the frosting. Place the second cake layer on top and frost the top and sides with the remaining frosting.
5. Decorate as desired and enjoy your delicious Canadian Carrot Cake!

This recipe captures the essence of Canadian carrot cake, perfect for any occasion with its moist texture and delightful cream cheese frosting.

Montreal Bagel Cake

Ingredients:

- **Cake Base:**
    - Use a dense, slightly sweetened cake base reminiscent of the chewy texture of Montreal bagels. A vanilla or cinnamon-flavored cake would work well.
- **Bagel-Inspired Flavors:**
    - Incorporate ingredients typically found in Montreal bagels, such as sesame seeds or poppy seeds, into the cake batter or as a crunchy topping.
- **Filling:**
    - Consider a filling inspired by cream cheese, which is a popular topping for Montreal bagels. A light cream cheese frosting or a cheesecake-like filling between layers could mimic this.
- **Topping:**
    - Sprinkle additional sesame seeds or poppy seeds on top of the cake for added texture and visual appeal, similar to the toppings on a bagel.
- **Decoration:**
    - Optionally, you can decorate the cake with mini Montreal bagels or bagel-shaped cookies for a whimsical touch that reflects the theme.

While this cake is more of a creative interpretation rather than a traditional recipe, it can be a fun and delicious way to celebrate the flavors of Montreal's iconic bagels in dessert form!

Prince Edward Island Potato Cake

Ingredients:

- 2 cups mashed potatoes (preferably Yukon Gold or similar creamy variety)
- 1 cup unsalted butter, softened
- 2 cups granulated sugar
- 4 large eggs
- 1 teaspoon vanilla extract
- 3 cups all-purpose flour
- 1 tablespoon baking powder
- 1/2 teaspoon salt
- 1 cup milk

Optional Glaze:

- 1 cup powdered sugar
- 2-3 tablespoons milk
- 1/2 teaspoon vanilla extract

Instructions:

1. Preheat your oven to 350°F (175°C). Grease and flour a 9x13-inch baking dish or two 9-inch round cake pans.
2. In a large mixing bowl, cream together the softened butter and sugar until light and fluffy.
3. Beat in the eggs, one at a time, and then add the vanilla extract.
4. In another bowl, whisk together the flour, baking powder, and salt.
5. Gradually add the dry ingredients to the creamed mixture, alternating with the mashed potatoes and milk. Begin and end with the dry ingredients, mixing until just combined after each addition.
6. Pour the batter into the prepared baking dish or pans, spreading evenly.
7. Bake in the preheated oven for 30-35 minutes (slightly longer if using a single baking dish), or until a toothpick inserted into the center comes out clean.
8. Remove from the oven and allow the cake to cool in the pan for 10 minutes before transferring to a wire rack to cool completely.

Optional Glaze:

1. In a small bowl, whisk together powdered sugar, milk, and vanilla extract until smooth.
2. Drizzle the glaze over the cooled cake.

This Prince Edward Island Potato Cake showcases the versatility of potatoes in a sweet, moist cake that's perfect for any occasion. Enjoy the unique flavors and the nod to PEI's agricultural heritage!

Niagara Peach Cake

Ingredients:

- 2 cups all-purpose flour
- 1 teaspoon baking powder
- 1/2 teaspoon baking soda
- 1/2 teaspoon salt
- 1/2 cup unsalted butter, softened
- 1 cup granulated sugar
- 2 large eggs
- 1 teaspoon vanilla extract
- 1/2 cup buttermilk
- 2 cups fresh Niagara peaches, peeled and diced
- 1/4 cup brown sugar (for topping)
- 1/2 teaspoon ground cinnamon (for topping)

Instructions:

1. Preheat your oven to 350°F (175°C). Grease and flour a 9-inch round cake pan or line it with parchment paper.
2. In a medium bowl, whisk together the flour, baking powder, baking soda, and salt.
3. In a large mixing bowl, cream together the softened butter and granulated sugar until light and fluffy.
4. Beat in the eggs, one at a time, and then add the vanilla extract.
5. Gradually add the dry ingredients to the creamed mixture, alternating with the buttermilk, beginning and ending with the dry ingredients. Mix until just combined.
6. Gently fold in the diced peaches.
7. Pour the batter into the prepared cake pan, spreading it evenly.
8. In a small bowl, mix together the brown sugar and ground cinnamon. Sprinkle this mixture evenly over the top of the cake batter.
9. Bake in the preheated oven for 40-45 minutes, or until a toothpick inserted into the center comes out clean.
10. Remove from the oven and let the cake cool in the pan for 10 minutes. Then, transfer it to a wire rack to cool completely.
11. Once cooled, slice and serve this delightful Niagara Peach Cake, savoring the flavors of fresh peaches in every bite.

This cake captures the essence of Niagara's delicious peaches, making it a perfect dessert to enjoy during peach season or any time you want to savor a taste of summer.

Alberta Wild Rose Cake

Ingredients:

- 2 cups all-purpose flour
- 1 teaspoon baking powder
- 1/2 teaspoon baking soda
- 1/2 teaspoon salt
- 1/2 cup unsalted butter, softened
- 1 cup granulated sugar
- 2 large eggs
- 1 teaspoon vanilla extract
- 1 cup buttermilk
- Zest of 1 lemon (optional, for added flavor)
- 1/2 cup wild rose petals (fresh or dried, finely chopped)
- 1/4 cup wild rose syrup or rose water (optional, for enhanced flavor)

Frosting:

- 8 oz (225g) cream cheese, softened
- 1/2 cup (115g) unsalted butter, softened
- 4 cups powdered sugar
- 1 teaspoon vanilla extract
- Wild rose petals, for decoration (optional)

Instructions:

1. Preheat your oven to 350°F (175°C). Grease and flour two 9-inch round cake pans or line them with parchment paper.
2. In a medium bowl, whisk together the flour, baking powder, baking soda, and salt.
3. In a large mixing bowl, cream together the softened butter and granulated sugar until light and fluffy.
4. Beat in the eggs, one at a time, and then add the vanilla extract and lemon zest (if using).
5. Gradually add the dry ingredients to the creamed mixture, alternating with the buttermilk, beginning and ending with the dry ingredients. Mix until just combined.
6. Gently fold in the chopped wild rose petals and rose syrup or rose water (if using).
7. Divide the batter evenly between the prepared cake pans.
8. Bake in the preheated oven for 25-30 minutes, or until a toothpick inserted into the center comes out clean.
9. Remove from the oven and let the cakes cool in the pans for 10 minutes. Then, transfer them to wire racks to cool completely.

For the Frosting:

1. In a large bowl, beat together the cream cheese and softened butter until smooth and creamy.
2. Gradually add the powdered sugar, one cup at a time, beating well after each addition.
3. Beat in the vanilla extract until smooth and creamy.

4. Once the cakes are completely cooled, frost the top of one cake layer with about 1/3 of the frosting. Place the second cake layer on top and frost the top and sides with the remaining frosting.
5. Decorate with wild rose petals if desired, and enjoy your Alberta Wild Rose Cake, celebrating the beauty of Alberta's provincial flower!

This cake not only captures the floral essence of Alberta's wild roses but also offers a delightful and unique flavor profile that's perfect for special occasions or simply to celebrate the natural beauty of the province.

Manitoba Morden Blush Cake

Ingredients:

- 2 cups cake flour
- 2 teaspoons baking powder
- 1/2 teaspoon baking soda
- 1/2 teaspoon salt
- 1/2 cup unsalted butter, softened
- 1 1/2 cups granulated sugar
- 3 large eggs
- 1 teaspoon vanilla extract
- 1 cup buttermilk
- Pink or blush food coloring (optional, for color)
- Edible rose petals (for garnish, optional)

Frosting:

- 8 oz (225g) cream cheese, softened
- 1/2 cup (115g) unsalted butter, softened
- 4 cups powdered sugar
- 1 teaspoon vanilla extract

Instructions:

1. Preheat your oven to 350°F (175°C). Grease and flour two 9-inch round cake pans or line them with parchment paper.
2. In a medium bowl, sift together the cake flour, baking powder, baking soda, and salt.
3. In a large mixing bowl, cream together the softened butter and granulated sugar until light and fluffy.
4. Add the eggs one at a time, beating well after each addition. Mix in the vanilla extract.
5. Gradually add the dry ingredients to the creamed mixture, alternating with the buttermilk, beginning and ending with the dry ingredients. Mix until just combined.
6. If desired, add a few drops of pink or blush food coloring to achieve the desired shade of blush.
7. Divide the batter evenly between the prepared cake pans.
8. Bake in the preheated oven for 25-30 minutes, or until a toothpick inserted into the center comes out clean.
9. Remove from the oven and let the cakes cool in the pans for 10 minutes. Then, transfer them to wire racks to cool completely.

For the Frosting:

1. In a large bowl, beat together the cream cheese and softened butter until smooth and creamy.
2. Gradually add the powdered sugar, one cup at a time, beating well after each addition.
3. Beat in the vanilla extract until smooth and creamy.
4. Once the cakes are completely cooled, frost the top of one cake layer with about 1/3 of the frosting. Place the second cake layer on top and frost the top and sides with the remaining frosting.
5. Optionally, garnish with edible rose petals for a beautiful finishing touch.

Enjoy this Manitoba Morden Blush Cake, inspired by the elegance of the Morden Blush rose and perfect for any special occasion or celebration!

British Columbia Apple Cake

Ingredients:

- 2 cups all-purpose flour
- 1 1/2 teaspoons baking powder
- 1/2 teaspoon baking soda
- 1/2 teaspoon salt
- 1 teaspoon ground cinnamon
- 1/2 teaspoon ground nutmeg
- 1/2 cup unsalted butter, softened
- 1 cup granulated sugar
- 2 large eggs
- 1 teaspoon vanilla extract
- 1/2 cup buttermilk
- 2 cups finely chopped apples (about 2 medium apples, peeled and cored)

Optional Topping:

- 1/4 cup brown sugar
- 1/2 teaspoon ground cinnamon
- 1/4 cup chopped walnuts or pecans (optional)

Instructions:

1. Preheat your oven to 350°F (175°C). Grease and flour a 9x13-inch baking dish or two 9-inch round cake pans.
2. In a medium bowl, whisk together the flour, baking powder, baking soda, salt, cinnamon, and nutmeg.
3. In a large mixing bowl, cream together the softened butter and granulated sugar until light and fluffy.
4. Beat in the eggs, one at a time, and then add the vanilla extract.
5. Gradually add the dry ingredients to the creamed mixture, alternating with the buttermilk, beginning and ending with the dry ingredients. Mix until just combined.
6. Gently fold in the chopped apples.
7. Pour the batter into the prepared baking dish or pans, spreading it evenly.
8. If using the optional topping, mix together the brown sugar, cinnamon, and chopped nuts (if using). Sprinkle evenly over the top of the cake batter.
9. Bake in the preheated oven for 30-35 minutes (slightly longer if using a single baking dish), or until a toothpick inserted into the center comes out clean.
10. Remove from the oven and let the cake cool in the pan for 10 minutes before transferring to a wire rack to cool completely.
11. Slice and serve this delightful British Columbia Apple Cake, celebrating the flavors of BC's fresh apples!

This cake is perfect for showcasing the delicious apples from British Columbia, offering a moist and flavorful dessert that's ideal for any occasion. Enjoy the taste of BC's orchards in every bite!

Canadian Butter Cake

Ingredients:

- 1 cup unsalted butter, softened
- 2 cups granulated sugar
- 4 large eggs
- 1 tablespoon vanilla extract
- 3 cups all-purpose flour
- 1 tablespoon baking powder
- 1/2 teaspoon salt
- 1 cup milk

Optional Glaze:

- 1 cup powdered sugar
- 2-3 tablespoons milk
- 1/2 teaspoon vanilla extract

Instructions:

1. Preheat your oven to 350°F (175°C). Grease and flour a 10-inch tube or bundt pan.
2. In a large mixing bowl, cream together the softened butter and granulated sugar until light and fluffy.
3. Beat in the eggs, one at a time, and then add the vanilla extract.
4. In a separate bowl, whisk together the flour, baking powder, and salt.
5. Gradually add the dry ingredients to the creamed mixture, alternating with the milk, beginning and ending with the dry ingredients. Mix until just combined.
6. Pour the batter into the prepared pan, spreading it evenly.
7. Bake in the preheated oven for 50-60 minutes, or until a toothpick inserted into the center comes out clean.
8. Remove from the oven and let the cake cool in the pan for 15 minutes. Then, invert the cake onto a wire rack to cool completely.

Optional Glaze:

1. In a small bowl, whisk together powdered sugar, milk, and vanilla extract until smooth.
2. Drizzle the glaze over the cooled cake.

This Canadian Butter Cake is perfect for those who love the rich flavor of butter in a moist and tender cake. It's a classic dessert that's sure to please any crowd, whether served on its own or with a dollop of whipped cream or fresh berries. Enjoy!

Butter Tart Bundt Cake

Ingredients:

- 1 cup unsalted butter, softened
- 1 1/2 cups packed brown sugar
- 3 large eggs
- 1 teaspoon vanilla extract
- 2 cups all-purpose flour
- 1 teaspoon baking powder
- 1/2 teaspoon baking soda
- 1/2 teaspoon salt
- 1 cup milk

Butter Tart Filling:

- 1/2 cup packed brown sugar
- 1/4 cup unsalted butter
- 1/4 cup maple syrup or corn syrup
- 1/4 cup heavy cream
- 1 teaspoon vanilla extract
- 1/2 cup chopped pecans or walnuts (optional)

Optional Glaze:

- 1/2 cup powdered sugar
- 2-3 tablespoons milk

Instructions:

1. Preheat your oven to 350°F (175°C). Grease and flour a 10-inch bundt pan.
2. In a large mixing bowl, cream together the softened butter and brown sugar until light and fluffy.
3. Beat in the eggs, one at a time, and then add the vanilla extract.
4. In a separate bowl, whisk together the flour, baking powder, baking soda, and salt.
5. Gradually add the dry ingredients to the creamed mixture, alternating with the milk, beginning and ending with the dry ingredients. Mix until just combined.
6. In a small saucepan, combine the brown sugar, butter, maple syrup or corn syrup, and heavy cream for the butter tart filling. Cook over medium heat, stirring constantly, until the mixture comes to a boil. Remove from heat and stir in the vanilla extract and chopped nuts (if using).
7. Pour half of the cake batter into the prepared bundt pan. Drizzle half of the butter tart filling over the batter. Repeat with the remaining batter and filling.
8. Bake in the preheated oven for 50-60 minutes, or until a toothpick inserted into the center comes out clean.
9. Remove from the oven and let the cake cool in the pan for 15 minutes. Then, invert the cake onto a wire rack to cool completely.

Optional Glaze:

1. In a small bowl, whisk together powdered sugar and milk until smooth. Drizzle the glaze over the cooled cake.

Serve this delicious Butter Tart Bundt Cake as a dessert or indulgent treat, capturing the flavors of Canadian butter tarts in a delightful cake form. Enjoy the rich caramel and nutty flavors with each bite!

Hudson's Bay Company Cake

Ingredients:

- 1 cup unsalted butter, softened
- 2 cups granulated sugar
- 4 large eggs
- 1 teaspoon vanilla extract
- 3 cups all-purpose flour
- 1 tablespoon baking powder
- 1/2 teaspoon salt
- 1 cup milk

Optional Topping:

- 1/4 cup unsalted butter
- 1/2 cup brown sugar
- 1/4 cup milk
- 1 cup sweetened shredded coconut

Instructions:

1. Preheat your oven to 350°F (175°C). Grease and flour a 9x13-inch baking dish or two 9-inch round cake pans.
2. In a large mixing bowl, cream together the softened butter and granulated sugar until light and fluffy.
3. Beat in the eggs, one at a time, and then add the vanilla extract.
4. In a separate bowl, whisk together the flour, baking powder, and salt.
5. Gradually add the dry ingredients to the creamed mixture, alternating with the milk, beginning and ending with the dry ingredients. Mix until just combined.
6. Pour the batter into the prepared baking dish or pans, spreading it evenly.
7. Bake in the preheated oven for 25-30 minutes (slightly longer if using a single baking dish), or until a toothpick inserted into the center comes out clean.
8. While the cake is baking, prepare the optional topping: In a saucepan, melt the butter over medium heat. Stir in the brown sugar and milk, and cook until the mixture comes to a boil. Remove from heat and stir in the shredded coconut.
9. Once the cake is baked, remove it from the oven and immediately spread the coconut topping evenly over the hot cake.
10. Return the cake to the oven and broil for 1-2 minutes, or until the topping is golden brown and bubbly. Watch carefully to prevent burning.
11. Remove from the oven and let the cake cool in the pan for 10 minutes. Then, transfer it to a wire rack to cool completely.

Enjoy this Hudson's Bay Company Cake, a delightful and nostalgic Canadian dessert that's perfect for sharing with friends and family!

Canadian Maple Walnut Cake

Ingredients:

- 1 cup unsalted butter, softened
- 1 cup granulated sugar
- 1 cup pure maple syrup
- 4 large eggs
- 1 teaspoon vanilla extract
- 2 cups all-purpose flour
- 1 teaspoon baking powder
- 1/2 teaspoon baking soda
- 1/2 teaspoon salt
- 1/2 cup buttermilk
- 1 cup chopped walnuts

Maple Buttercream Frosting:

- 1 cup unsalted butter, softened
- 3 cups powdered sugar
- 1/4 cup pure maple syrup
- 1 teaspoon vanilla extract
- Chopped walnuts, for garnish (optional)

Instructions:

1. Preheat your oven to 350°F (175°C). Grease and flour two 9-inch round cake pans.
2. In a large mixing bowl, cream together the softened butter and granulated sugar until light and fluffy.
3. Beat in the maple syrup, eggs (one at a time), and vanilla extract until well combined.
4. In a separate bowl, whisk together the flour, baking powder, baking soda, and salt.
5. Gradually add the dry ingredients to the wet mixture, alternating with the buttermilk, beginning and ending with the dry ingredients. Mix until just combined.
6. Fold in the chopped walnuts.
7. Divide the batter evenly between the prepared cake pans.
8. Bake in the preheated oven for 25-30 minutes, or until a toothpick inserted into the center comes out clean.
9. Remove from the oven and let the cakes cool in the pans for 10 minutes. Then, transfer them to wire racks to cool completely.

Maple Buttercream Frosting:

1. In a large bowl, beat the softened butter until creamy.
2. Gradually add the powdered sugar, one cup at a time, beating well after each addition.
3. Beat in the maple syrup and vanilla extract until smooth and fluffy.
4. Once the cakes are completely cooled, frost the top of one cake layer with a generous amount of maple buttercream frosting. Place the second cake layer on top and frost the top and sides with the remaining frosting.
5. Optionally, garnish with chopped walnuts on top of the cake.

Slice and serve this Canadian Maple Walnut Cake to enjoy the wonderful combination of maple syrup sweetness and crunchy walnuts, perfect for any occasion or celebration!

Quebec Sugar Pie Cake

Ingredients:

For the Cake:

- 1 cup unsalted butter, softened
- 1 cup granulated sugar
- 4 large eggs
- 1 teaspoon vanilla extract
- 2 cups all-purpose flour
- 1 teaspoon baking powder
- 1/2 teaspoon baking soda
- 1/2 teaspoon salt
- 1 cup buttermilk

For the Sugar Pie Filling:

- 1 cup brown sugar
- 1 cup pure maple syrup
- 1/2 cup heavy cream
- 1/4 cup unsalted butter
- 1 teaspoon vanilla extract
- Pinch of salt

Optional Topping:

- Whipped cream or vanilla ice cream, for serving

Instructions:

1. **Preheat** your oven to 350°F (175°C). Grease and flour a 9x13-inch baking dish or two 9-inch round cake pans.
2. **Prepare** the Sugar Pie Filling: In a saucepan over medium heat, combine the brown sugar, maple syrup, heavy cream, butter, vanilla extract, and salt. Stir continuously until the mixture comes to a gentle boil. Reduce the heat to low and simmer for 5 minutes, stirring occasionally. Remove from heat and let it cool slightly.
3. **For the Cake Batter:** In a large mixing bowl, cream together the softened butter and granulated sugar until light and fluffy. Beat in the eggs, one at a time, and then add the vanilla extract.
4. **In another bowl,** whisk together the flour, baking powder, baking soda, and salt.
5. **Gradually add** the dry ingredients to the creamed mixture, alternating with the buttermilk, beginning and ending with the dry ingredients. Mix until just combined.
6. **Pour** half of the cake batter into the prepared baking dish or pans, spreading it evenly.
7. **Drizzle** half of the prepared Sugar Pie Filling over the batter. Repeat with the remaining batter and filling.
8. **Bake** in the preheated oven for 30-35 minutes (slightly longer if using a single baking dish), or until a toothpick inserted into the center comes out clean.
9. **Remove** from the oven and let the cake cool in the pan for 10 minutes before transferring it to a wire rack to cool completely.

10. **Serve** slices of this Quebec Sugar Pie Cake warm or at room temperature, optionally topped with whipped cream or vanilla ice cream.

This cake celebrates the rich flavors of Quebec's sugar pie in a delightful cake form, perfect for sharing with friends and family during any special occasion or holiday gathering. Enjoy the sweet taste of Québécois tradition!

Toronto Blueberry Cheesecake Cake

Ingredients:

For the Cake Layers:

- 2 cups all-purpose flour
- 2 teaspoons baking powder
- 1/2 teaspoon baking soda
- 1/2 teaspoon salt
- 1/2 cup unsalted butter, softened
- 1 cup granulated sugar
- 2 large eggs
- 1 teaspoon vanilla extract
- 1 cup buttermilk

For the Blueberry Compote:

- 2 cups fresh or frozen blueberries
- 1/4 cup granulated sugar
- 1 tablespoon lemon juice
- 1 tablespoon cornstarch mixed with 1 tablespoon water (optional, for thickening)

For the Cheesecake Layer:

- 16 oz (450g) cream cheese, softened
- 1/2 cup granulated sugar
- 1 teaspoon vanilla extract
- 2 large eggs

For the Cream Cheese Frosting:

- 8 oz (225g) cream cheese, softened
- 1/2 cup unsalted butter, softened
- 4 cups powdered sugar
- 1 teaspoon vanilla extract

Instructions:

1. **Preheat** your oven to 350°F (175°C). Grease and flour three 9-inch round cake pans.
2. **Prepare the Cake Layers:**
    - In a medium bowl, whisk together the flour, baking powder, baking soda, and salt.
    - In a large mixing bowl, cream together the softened butter and granulated sugar until light and fluffy.
    - Beat in the eggs, one at a time, and then add the vanilla extract.
    - Gradually add the dry ingredients to the creamed mixture, alternating with the buttermilk, beginning and ending with the dry ingredients. Mix until just combined.
    - Divide the batter evenly between the prepared cake pans.
    - Bake in the preheated oven for 20-25 minutes, or until a toothpick inserted into the center comes out clean.

- Remove from the oven and let the cakes cool in the pans for 10 minutes before transferring them to wire racks to cool completely.
3. **Prepare the Blueberry Compote:**
    - In a saucepan, combine the blueberries, granulated sugar, and lemon juice. Cook over medium heat until the blueberries burst and release their juices, stirring occasionally.
    - If desired, thicken the compote by stirring in the cornstarch mixture and simmer for an additional 1-2 minutes. Remove from heat and let it cool completely.
4. **Prepare the Cheesecake Layer:**
    - In a large bowl, beat the softened cream cheese until smooth.
    - Gradually add the granulated sugar and beat until well combined.
    - Beat in the vanilla extract and eggs, one at a time, until smooth and creamy.
5. **Assemble the Cake:**
    - Place one cooled cake layer on a serving plate or cake stand.
    - Spread half of the cooled blueberry compote evenly over the cake layer.
    - Carefully spread half of the cheesecake batter over the blueberry compote.
    - Repeat with the second cake layer, remaining blueberry compote, and remaining cheesecake batter.
    - Top with the third cake layer.
6. **Prepare the Cream Cheese Frosting:**
    - In a large bowl, beat together the softened cream cheese and butter until smooth and creamy.
    - Gradually add the powdered sugar, one cup at a time, beating well after each addition.
    - Beat in the vanilla extract until smooth and fluffy.
7. **Frost the Cake:**
    - Frost the top and sides of the assembled cake with the cream cheese frosting.
    - Optionally, garnish with fresh blueberries or additional blueberry compote.
8. **Chill** the cake in the refrigerator for at least 1 hour before serving to allow the flavors to meld together.

Enjoy this Toronto Blueberry Cheesecake Cake, a delightful combination of cheesecake and blueberry goodness that's perfect for any celebration or special occasion!

Nova Scotia Blueberry Grunt Cake

Ingredients:

For the Blueberry Filling:

- 4 cups fresh or frozen blueberries
- 1/2 cup granulated sugar
- 1 tablespoon lemon juice
- 1 teaspoon vanilla extract
- 1/2 teaspoon ground cinnamon
- 1/4 teaspoon ground nutmeg
- Zest of 1 lemon
- 2 tablespoons cornstarch mixed with 2 tablespoons water

For the Biscuit Topping:

- 2 cups all-purpose flour
- 1/4 cup granulated sugar
- 1 tablespoon baking powder
- 1/2 teaspoon baking soda
- 1/2 teaspoon salt
- 1/2 cup unsalted butter, cold and cut into small pieces
- 1 cup buttermilk

For Serving (Optional):

- Vanilla ice cream or whipped cream

Instructions:

1. **Preheat** your oven to 375°F (190°C). Grease a 9x13-inch baking dish or similar-sized casserole dish.
2. **Prepare the Blueberry Filling:**
    - In a large bowl, combine the blueberries, granulated sugar, lemon juice, vanilla extract, ground cinnamon, ground nutmeg, and lemon zest.
    - Stir in the cornstarch mixture until well combined.
    - Transfer the blueberry mixture to the prepared baking dish, spreading it evenly.
3. **Prepare the Biscuit Topping:**
    - In a large bowl, whisk together the flour, granulated sugar, baking powder, baking soda, and salt.
    - Cut in the cold butter pieces using a pastry cutter or your fingertips until the mixture resembles coarse crumbs.
    - Gradually add the buttermilk, stirring with a fork until the dough just comes together.
4. **Assemble and Bake:**
    - Drop spoonfuls of the biscuit topping evenly over the blueberry filling in the baking dish.
    - Bake in the preheated oven for 35-40 minutes, or until the biscuit topping is golden brown and the blueberry filling is bubbly.
5. **Serve Warm:**

- Remove from the oven and let it cool for a few minutes.
- Serve the Nova Scotia Blueberry Grunt Cake warm, optionally topped with vanilla ice cream or whipped cream.

Enjoy this comforting and flavorful dessert that showcases the sweetness of Nova Scotia blueberries with a delightful biscuit topping, perfect for sharing with family and friends!

Newfoundland Jam Jam Cake

Ingredients:

For the Cake:

- 1/2 cup unsalted butter, softened
- 1 cup granulated sugar
- 2 large eggs
- 1 teaspoon vanilla extract
- 1 1/2 cups all-purpose flour
- 1 teaspoon baking powder
- 1/2 teaspoon baking soda
- 1/4 teaspoon salt
- 1/2 cup buttermilk

For the Jam Filling:

- 1 cup your favorite jam (such as raspberry or strawberry)

For the Icing:

- 2 cups powdered sugar
- 2-3 tablespoons water or milk
- 1/2 teaspoon vanilla extract

Instructions:

1. **Preheat** your oven to 350°F (175°C). Grease and flour a 9x13-inch baking dish or two 9-inch round cake pans.
2. **Prepare the Cake:**
    - In a large mixing bowl, cream together the softened butter and granulated sugar until light and fluffy.
    - Beat in the eggs, one at a time, and then add the vanilla extract.
    - In a separate bowl, whisk together the flour, baking powder, baking soda, and salt.
    - Gradually add the dry ingredients to the creamed mixture, alternating with the buttermilk, beginning and ending with the dry ingredients. Mix until just combined.
    - Pour the batter into the prepared baking dish or pans, spreading it evenly.
3. **Bake** in the preheated oven for 20-25 minutes (slightly longer if using a single baking dish), or until a toothpick inserted into the center comes out clean.
4. **Prepare the Jam Filling:**
    - Once the cake is baked and cooled slightly, spread the jam evenly over the top of the cake.
5. **Prepare the Icing:**
    - In a small bowl, whisk together the powdered sugar, water or milk, and vanilla extract until smooth and pourable.
    - Drizzle the icing over the jam-covered cake.
6. **Serve:** Slice and serve this delightful Newfoundland Jam Jam Cake, enjoying the flavors reminiscent of the classic Newfoundland Jam Jams cookies in a cake form.

This cake is perfect for any occasion, capturing the sweet and fruity essence of Newfoundland's favorite treat. Enjoy the taste of Jam Jams in a new and delightful way!

Yukon Gold Rush Cake

Ingredients:

For the Cake:

- 2 cups all-purpose flour
- 1 teaspoon baking powder
- 1/2 teaspoon baking soda
- 1/2 teaspoon salt
- 1/2 cup unsalted butter, softened
- 1 cup granulated sugar
- 2 large eggs
- 1 teaspoon vanilla extract
- 1 cup buttermilk

For the Filling:

- 1 cup Yukon gold potatoes, cooked, mashed, and cooled
- 1/2 cup brown sugar
- 1/2 cup chopped walnuts or pecans
- 1 teaspoon ground cinnamon
- 1/2 teaspoon ground nutmeg
- 1/4 teaspoon ground cloves

For the Frosting:

- 8 oz cream cheese, softened
- 1/2 cup unsalted butter, softened
- 3 cups powdered sugar
- 1 teaspoon vanilla extract

Optional Garnish:

- Chopped nuts or edible gold flakes

Instructions:

1. **Preheat** your oven to 350°F (175°C). Grease and flour two 9-inch round cake pans.
2. **Prepare the Cake:**
   - In a medium bowl, whisk together the flour, baking powder, baking soda, and salt.
   - In a large mixing bowl, cream together the softened butter and granulated sugar until light and fluffy.
   - Beat in the eggs, one at a time, and then add the vanilla extract.
   - Gradually add the dry ingredients to the creamed mixture, alternating with the buttermilk, beginning and ending with the dry ingredients. Mix until just combined.
   - Divide the batter evenly between the prepared cake pans.
   - Bake in the preheated oven for 20-25 minutes, or until a toothpick inserted into the center comes out clean.

- Remove from the oven and let the cakes cool in the pans for 10 minutes before transferring them to wire racks to cool completely.

3. **Prepare the Filling:**
    - In a bowl, combine the cooked and mashed Yukon gold potatoes with brown sugar, chopped nuts, cinnamon, nutmeg, and cloves. Mix until well combined.
4. **Prepare the Frosting:**
    - In a large bowl, beat together the softened cream cheese and butter until smooth and creamy.
    - Gradually add the powdered sugar, one cup at a time, beating well after each addition.
    - Beat in the vanilla extract until smooth and fluffy.
5. **Assemble the Cake:**
    - Place one cooled cake layer on a serving plate or cake stand.
    - Spread the Yukon gold potato filling evenly over the cake layer.
    - Place the second cake layer on top.
    - Frost the top and sides of the cake with the cream cheese frosting.
6. **Optional Garnish:**
    - Sprinkle chopped nuts or edible gold flakes on top of the cake for a decorative touch.
7. **Serve and Enjoy:** Slice and serve this unique Yukon Gold Rush Cake, celebrating the flavors and history associated with the Yukon region and the Gold Rush era.

This cake is sure to be a conversation starter and a delicious treat that pays homage to the historical significance of the Yukon Gold Rush.

Banff Rocky Road Cake

Ingredients:

- 1 and 1/2 cups all-purpose flour
- 1/2 cup unsweetened cocoa powder
- 1 teaspoon baking powder
- 1/2 teaspoon baking soda
- 1/4 teaspoon salt
- 1/2 cup unsalted butter, softened
- 1 cup granulated sugar
- 2 large eggs
- 1 teaspoon vanilla extract
- 1/2 cup buttermilk
- 1 cup mini marshmallows
- 1/2 cup chopped almonds or walnuts
- 1/2 cup chocolate chips or chunks
- 1 cup marshmallow fluff (marshmallow cream)

Instructions:

1. **Preheat** your oven to 350°F (175°C). Grease and flour a 9-inch round cake pan or line it with parchment paper.
2. **Mix dry ingredients**: In a medium bowl, whisk together the flour, cocoa powder, baking powder, baking soda, and salt. Set aside.
3. **Cream butter and sugar**: In a large bowl, beat the softened butter and sugar until light and fluffy, about 2-3 minutes.
4. **Add eggs and vanilla**: Beat in the eggs, one at a time, then add the vanilla extract. Mix until well combined.
5. **Combine wet and dry ingredients**: Gradually add the flour mixture to the butter mixture, alternating with buttermilk, beginning and ending with the flour mixture. Mix until just combined.
6. **Fold in mix-ins**: Gently fold in the mini marshmallows, chopped nuts, and chocolate chips or chunks until evenly distributed in the batter.
7. **Bake**: Pour the batter into the prepared cake pan and smooth the top. Bake in the preheated oven for 30-35 minutes, or until a toothpick inserted into the center comes out clean.
8. **Cool**: Remove the cake from the oven and let it cool in the pan for 10 minutes. Then, transfer it to a wire rack to cool completely.
9. **Top with marshmallow fluff**: Once the cake has cooled, spread the marshmallow fluff evenly over the top of the cake. You can toast the marshmallow fluff lightly with a kitchen torch for a more traditional rocky road effect.
10. **Serve**: Slice and serve your delicious Banff Rocky Road Cake! Enjoy the chocolatey, marshmallowy goodness.

This recipe captures the essence of a rocky road dessert with its mix of textures and flavors. It's perfect for chocolate lovers and those who enjoy a bit of nostalgic indulgence in their desserts.

Vancouver Island Blackberry Cake

Ingredients:

- 1 and 1/2 cups all-purpose flour
- 1 teaspoon baking powder
- 1/2 teaspoon baking soda
- 1/4 teaspoon salt
- 1/2 cup unsalted butter, softened
- 3/4 cup granulated sugar
- 2 large eggs
- 1 teaspoon vanilla extract
- 1/2 cup sour cream
- 1/2 cup milk
- 1 and 1/2 cups fresh blackberries (or frozen, thawed and drained)
- Powdered sugar, for dusting (optional)

Instructions:

1. **Preheat** your oven to 350°F (175°C). Grease and flour a 9-inch round cake pan or line it with parchment paper.
2. **Mix dry ingredients**: In a medium bowl, whisk together the flour, baking powder, baking soda, and salt. Set aside.
3. **Cream butter and sugar**: In a large bowl, beat the softened butter and granulated sugar until light and fluffy, about 2-3 minutes.
4. **Add eggs and vanilla**: Beat in the eggs, one at a time, then add the vanilla extract. Mix until well combined.
5. **Combine wet and dry ingredients**: Gradually add the flour mixture to the butter mixture, alternating with the sour cream and milk, beginning and ending with the flour mixture. Mix until just combined.
6. **Fold in blackberries**: Gently fold in the fresh blackberries until evenly distributed in the batter.
7. **Bake**: Pour the batter into the prepared cake pan and smooth the top. Bake in the preheated oven for 30-35 minutes, or until a toothpick inserted into the center comes out clean.
8. **Cool**: Remove the cake from the oven and let it cool in the pan for 10 minutes. Then, transfer it to a wire rack to cool completely.
9. **Dust with powdered sugar**: Once cooled, dust the top of the cake with powdered sugar if desired.
10. **Serve**: Slice and serve your Vancouver Island Blackberry Cake! This cake showcases the sweet-tart flavor of fresh blackberries, perfect for a summer treat.

This recipe captures the essence of Vancouver Island's bounty of blackberries, making it a delightful dessert that highlights local flavors. Enjoy the moist and flavorful cake with bursts of juicy blackberries in every bite!

Ottawa Beaver Tail Cake

Ingredients:

- **For the Dough:**
    - 2 cups all-purpose flour
    - 1/2 cup whole wheat flour
    - 1/4 cup granulated sugar
    - 1 packet (2 1/4 tsp) active dry yeast
    - 1/2 tsp salt
    - 3/4 cup warm milk (110°F)
    - 1/4 cup warm water (110°F)
    - 1/4 cup unsalted butter, melted
    - 1 large egg
    - 1 tsp vanilla extract
- **For Frying:**
    - Vegetable oil for frying
- **For Topping:**
    - 1 cup granulated sugar
    - 2 tsp ground cinnamon
    - Optional toppings: lemon juice, chocolate hazelnut spread, maple syrup, whipped cream, fresh fruit, etc.

Instructions:

1. **Prepare the Dough:**
    - In a large bowl, combine the all-purpose flour, whole wheat flour, granulated sugar, yeast, and salt.
    - In a separate bowl, mix the warm milk, warm water, melted butter, egg, and vanilla extract.
    - Gradually add the wet ingredients to the dry ingredients, mixing until a soft dough forms.
    - Knead the dough on a lightly floured surface for about 5-7 minutes until smooth and elastic.
    - Place the dough in a greased bowl, cover with a damp cloth, and let it rise in a warm place for about 1 hour or until doubled in size.
2. **Shape and Fry the Dough:**
    - Punch down the risen dough and divide it into 10-12 equal pieces.
    - Roll each piece into an oval shape, about 1/4 inch thick.
    - Heat the vegetable oil in a deep fryer or large pot to 375°F (190°C).
    - Carefully place the dough ovals into the hot oil, frying them one or two at a time for about 1-2 minutes per side, or until golden brown and puffed.
    - Use a slotted spoon to transfer the fried dough to a paper towel-lined plate to drain excess oil.
3. **Add the Topping:**
    - In a shallow bowl, mix the granulated sugar and ground cinnamon.
    - While the beaver tails are still warm, coat them in the cinnamon-sugar mixture.
    - Serve immediately with optional toppings like lemon juice, chocolate hazelnut spread, maple syrup, whipped cream, or fresh fruit.

Enjoy your homemade Ottawa Beaver Tail Cake!

Quebec Maple Buttercream Cake

Ingredients:

- **For the Cake:**
    - 2 1/2 cups all-purpose flour
    - 2 1/2 tsp baking powder
    - 1/2 tsp salt
    - 1 cup unsalted butter, room temperature
    - 1 1/2 cups granulated sugar
    - 4 large eggs, room temperature
    - 2 tsp vanilla extract
    - 1 cup whole milk, room temperature
    - 1/2 cup pure maple syrup
- **For the Maple Buttercream:**
    - 1 cup unsalted butter, room temperature
    - 3 1/2 cups powdered sugar
    - 1/4 cup pure maple syrup
    - 1-2 tbsp heavy cream
    - 1 tsp vanilla extract
    - Pinch of salt

Instructions:

1. **Prepare the Cake:**
    - Preheat your oven to 350°F (175°C). Grease and flour two 9-inch round cake pans.
    - In a medium bowl, whisk together the flour, baking powder, and salt.
    - In a large bowl, beat the butter and granulated sugar together until light and fluffy, about 3-5 minutes.
    - Add the eggs one at a time, beating well after each addition. Mix in the vanilla extract.
    - In a small bowl, combine the milk and maple syrup.
    - Gradually add the flour mixture to the butter mixture, alternating with the milk and maple syrup mixture, beginning and ending with the flour mixture. Mix until just combined.
    - Divide the batter evenly between the prepared cake pans and smooth the tops.
    - Bake for 25-30 minutes, or until a toothpick inserted into the center of the cakes comes out clean.
    - Let the cakes cool in the pans for 10 minutes, then remove from the pans and transfer to a wire rack to cool completely.
2. **Prepare the Maple Buttercream:**
    - In a large bowl, beat the butter until creamy and smooth, about 2-3 minutes.
    - Gradually add the powdered sugar, one cup at a time, beating well after each addition.
    - Add the maple syrup, heavy cream, vanilla extract, and salt. Beat on high speed for 3-4 minutes, until the buttercream is light and fluffy.
    - If the buttercream is too thick, add an additional tablespoon of heavy cream. If it's too thin, add more powdered sugar, one tablespoon at a time, until the desired consistency is reached.
3. **Assemble the Cake:**
    - Place one cake layer on a serving plate or cake stand. Spread a generous layer of maple buttercream over the top.

- Place the second cake layer on top of the buttercream, pressing down lightly.
- Frost the top and sides of the cake with the remaining maple buttercream.
- Optionally, drizzle additional maple syrup over the top of the cake for extra maple flavor.
4. **Serve and Enjoy:**
    - Allow the cake to set for about 30 minutes before slicing.
    - Enjoy your delicious Quebec Maple Buttercream Cake with friends and family!

This cake is a delightful blend of rich, buttery layers with the sweet, distinctive taste of maple syrup, making it a perfect treat for any occasion.

Calgary Stampede Cake

Ingredients:

- **For the Cake:**
    - 2 1/2 cups all-purpose flour
    - 2 1/2 tsp baking powder
    - 1/2 tsp salt
    - 1 cup unsalted butter, room temperature
    - 1 1/2 cups granulated sugar
    - 4 large eggs, room temperature
    - 2 tsp vanilla extract
    - 1 cup whole milk, room temperature
    - 1/2 cup buttermilk, room temperature
- **For the Cinnamon Sugar Swirl:**
    - 1/2 cup light brown sugar, packed
    - 1/4 cup granulated sugar
    - 2 tsp ground cinnamon
    - 1/4 cup unsalted butter, melted
- **For the Maple Pecan Topping:**
    - 1/2 cup unsalted butter
    - 1 cup light brown sugar, packed
    - 1/2 cup pure maple syrup
    - 1/4 cup heavy cream
    - 1 cup chopped pecans

Instructions:

1. **Prepare the Cake:**
    - Preheat your oven to 350°F (175°C). Grease and flour a 9x13-inch baking pan.
    - In a medium bowl, whisk together the flour, baking powder, and salt.
    - In a large bowl, beat the butter and granulated sugar together until light and fluffy, about 3-5 minutes.
    - Add the eggs one at a time, beating well after each addition. Mix in the vanilla extract.
    - In a small bowl, combine the whole milk and buttermilk.
    - Gradually add the flour mixture to the butter mixture, alternating with the milk and buttermilk mixture, beginning and ending with the flour mixture. Mix until just combined.
    - Pour half of the batter into the prepared baking pan and spread it evenly.
2. **Prepare the Cinnamon Sugar Swirl:**
    - In a small bowl, mix together the brown sugar, granulated sugar, and ground cinnamon.
    - Sprinkle the cinnamon sugar mixture evenly over the batter in the pan.
    - Drizzle the melted butter over the cinnamon sugar mixture.
    - Pour the remaining batter over the cinnamon sugar layer and spread it evenly to cover.
3. **Bake the Cake:**
    - Bake for 30-35 minutes, or until a toothpick inserted into the center of the cake comes out clean.
    - Let the cake cool in the pan on a wire rack.
4. **Prepare the Maple Pecan Topping:**
    - In a medium saucepan, melt the butter over medium heat.

- Add the brown sugar, maple syrup, and heavy cream, stirring constantly until the mixture comes to a boil.
- Continue to boil for 2-3 minutes, then remove from heat and stir in the chopped pecans.
- Allow the topping to cool slightly, then pour it over the cooled cake, spreading it evenly.

5. **Serve and Enjoy:**
    - Allow the cake to set for about 15 minutes before slicing.
    - Enjoy your Calgary Stampede Cake with friends and family!

This cake captures the spirit of the Calgary Stampede with its rich, buttery layers, sweet cinnamon swirl, and decadent maple pecan topping, making it a perfect treat for any occasion.

Ontario Black Forest Cake

Ingredients:

- **For the Cake:**
    - 1 3/4 cups all-purpose flour
    - 3/4 cup unsweetened cocoa powder
    - 2 cups granulated sugar
    - 1 1/2 tsp baking powder
    - 1 1/2 tsp baking soda
    - 1 tsp salt
    - 2 large eggs, room temperature
    - 1 cup whole milk, room temperature
    - 1/2 cup vegetable oil
    - 2 tsp vanilla extract
    - 1 cup boiling water
- **For the Cherry Filling:**
    - 2 cups pitted sweet cherries (fresh or frozen)
    - 1/2 cup granulated sugar
    - 2 tbsp cornstarch
    - 1/4 cup water
    - 2 tbsp kirsch (cherry brandy) or cherry juice
- **For the Whipped Cream Frosting:**
    - 2 cups heavy whipping cream
    - 1/2 cup powdered sugar
    - 1 tsp vanilla extract
- **For Garnish:**
    - Chocolate shavings or curls
    - Fresh cherries

Instructions:

1. **Prepare the Cake:**
    - Preheat your oven to 350°F (175°C). Grease and flour two 9-inch round cake pans.
    - In a large bowl, whisk together the flour, cocoa powder, granulated sugar, baking powder, baking soda, and salt.
    - Add the eggs, milk, vegetable oil, and vanilla extract. Beat on medium speed for 2 minutes.
    - Stir in the boiling water (the batter will be thin).
    - Pour the batter evenly into the prepared cake pans.
    - Bake for 30-35 minutes, or until a toothpick inserted into the center comes out clean.
    - Cool the cakes in the pans for 10 minutes, then remove them from the pans and transfer to a wire rack to cool completely.
2. **Prepare the Cherry Filling:**
    - In a medium saucepan, combine the pitted cherries, granulated sugar, cornstarch, and water.
    - Cook over medium heat, stirring constantly, until the mixture thickens and boils.
    - Remove from heat and stir in the kirsch or cherry juice.
    - Let the cherry filling cool completely.

3. **Prepare the Whipped Cream Frosting:**
   - In a large bowl, beat the heavy whipping cream, powdered sugar, and vanilla extract on high speed until stiff peaks form.
4. **Assemble the Cake:**
   - Place one cake layer on a serving plate or cake stand. Spread a layer of cherry filling over the cake layer.
   - Spread a layer of whipped cream frosting over the cherry filling.
   - Place the second cake layer on top, pressing down lightly.
   - Spread the remaining whipped cream frosting over the top and sides of the cake.
   - Garnish with chocolate shavings or curls and fresh cherries.
5. **Serve and Enjoy:**
   - Chill the cake in the refrigerator for at least 1 hour before serving to allow the flavors to meld.
   - Slice and enjoy your Ontario Black Forest Cake with friends and family!

This cake combines the rich, chocolatey layers with a sweet cherry filling and light whipped cream frosting, making it a delightful treat inspired by the flavors of Ontario.

British Columbia Rainforest Cake

Ingredients:

- **For the Cake:**
    - 2 1/2 cups all-purpose flour
    - 2 tsp baking powder
    - 1/2 tsp baking soda
    - 1/2 tsp salt
    - 1/2 cup unsweetened cocoa powder
    - 1 1/2 cups granulated sugar
    - 3/4 cup vegetable oil
    - 3 large eggs, room temperature
    - 1 tsp vanilla extract
    - 1 cup buttermilk, room temperature
    - 1/2 cup strong brewed coffee, cooled
- **For the Berry Compote:**
    - 2 cups mixed berries (blueberries, blackberries, raspberries)
    - 1/2 cup granulated sugar
    - 2 tbsp lemon juice
    - 2 tbsp cornstarch
    - 1/4 cup water
- **For the Chocolate Ganache:**
    - 1 cup heavy cream
    - 8 oz dark chocolate, chopped
    - 2 tbsp unsalted butter
- **For the Decoration:**
    - Fresh berries (blueberries, blackberries, raspberries)
    - Edible flowers (optional)

Instructions:

1. **Prepare the Cake:**
    - Preheat your oven to 350°F (175°C). Grease and flour two 9-inch round cake pans.
    - In a medium bowl, whisk together the flour, baking powder, baking soda, salt, and cocoa powder.
    - In a large bowl, beat the sugar and vegetable oil together until well combined.
    - Add the eggs one at a time, beating well after each addition. Mix in the vanilla extract.
    - Gradually add the flour mixture to the wet ingredients, alternating with the buttermilk, beginning and ending with the flour mixture.
    - Stir in the cooled coffee until the batter is smooth.
    - Divide the batter evenly between the prepared cake pans and smooth the tops.
    - Bake for 30-35 minutes, or until a toothpick inserted into the center of the cakes comes out clean.
    - Let the cakes cool in the pans for 10 minutes, then remove from the pans and transfer to a wire rack to cool completely.
2. **Prepare the Berry Compote:**
    - In a medium saucepan, combine the mixed berries, granulated sugar, and lemon juice.

- Cook over medium heat until the berries release their juices and the mixture comes to a boil.
- In a small bowl, mix the cornstarch and water until smooth. Stir the cornstarch mixture into the berry mixture.
- Continue to cook, stirring constantly, until the mixture thickens, about 2-3 minutes.
- Remove from heat and let the compote cool completely.

3. **Prepare the Chocolate Ganache:**
    - In a small saucepan, heat the heavy cream over medium heat until it just begins to simmer.
    - Remove from heat and add the chopped dark chocolate and butter.
    - Let the mixture sit for 2-3 minutes, then stir until smooth and glossy.
    - Allow the ganache to cool slightly until it thickens to a pourable consistency.
4. **Assemble the Cake:**
    - Place one cake layer on a serving plate or cake stand. Spread a layer of berry compote over the cake layer.
    - Place the second cake layer on top, pressing down lightly.
    - Pour the chocolate ganache over the top of the cake, letting it drip down the sides.
    - Decorate with fresh berries and edible flowers, if desired.
5. **Serve and Enjoy:**
    - Chill the cake in the refrigerator for about 30 minutes to set the ganache.
    - Slice and enjoy your British Columbia Rainforest Cake with friends and family!

This cake combines the rich flavors of chocolate and coffee with the fresh, vibrant taste of mixed berries, capturing the essence of the lush, diverse landscapes of British Columbia.

Quebec Maple Pecan Cake

Ingredients:

- **For the Cake:**
    - 2 1/2 cups all-purpose flour
    - 2 tsp baking powder
    - 1/2 tsp baking soda
    - 1/2 tsp salt
    - 1 cup unsalted butter, room temperature
    - 1 1/2 cups granulated sugar
    - 4 large eggs, room temperature
    - 1 tsp vanilla extract
    - 1/2 cup pure maple syrup
    - 1 cup buttermilk, room temperature
    - 1 cup chopped pecans
- **For the Maple Buttercream:**
    - 1 cup unsalted butter, room temperature
    - 3 1/2 cups powdered sugar
    - 1/4 cup pure maple syrup
    - 1-2 tbsp heavy cream
    - 1 tsp vanilla extract
    - Pinch of salt
- **For the Pecan Caramel Sauce:**
    - 1/2 cup unsalted butter
    - 1 cup light brown sugar, packed
    - 1/2 cup heavy cream
    - 1/4 cup pure maple syrup
    - 1 tsp vanilla extract
    - 1 cup chopped pecans

Instructions:

1. **Prepare the Cake:**
    - Preheat your oven to 350°F (175°C). Grease and flour two 9-inch round cake pans.
    - In a medium bowl, whisk together the flour, baking powder, baking soda, and salt.
    - In a large bowl, beat the butter and granulated sugar together until light and fluffy, about 3-5 minutes.
    - Add the eggs one at a time, beating well after each addition. Mix in the vanilla extract and maple syrup.
    - Gradually add the flour mixture to the butter mixture, alternating with the buttermilk, beginning and ending with the flour mixture. Mix until just combined.
    - Fold in the chopped pecans.
    - Divide the batter evenly between the prepared cake pans and smooth the tops.
    - Bake for 25-30 minutes, or until a toothpick inserted into the center of the cakes comes out clean.
    - Let the cakes cool in the pans for 10 minutes, then remove from the pans and transfer to a wire rack to cool completely.
2. **Prepare the Maple Buttercream:**

- In a large bowl, beat the butter until creamy and smooth, about 2-3 minutes.
- Gradually add the powdered sugar, one cup at a time, beating well after each addition.
- Add the maple syrup, heavy cream, vanilla extract, and salt. Beat on high speed for 3-4 minutes, until the buttercream is light and fluffy.
- If the buttercream is too thick, add an additional tablespoon of heavy cream. If it's too thin, add more powdered sugar, one tablespoon at a time, until the desired consistency is reached.

3. **Prepare the Pecan Caramel Sauce:**
   - In a medium saucepan, melt the butter over medium heat.
   - Add the brown sugar, heavy cream, and maple syrup, stirring constantly until the mixture comes to a boil.
   - Continue to boil for 2-3 minutes, then remove from heat and stir in the vanilla extract and chopped pecans.
   - Allow the sauce to cool slightly before using.

4. **Assemble the Cake:**
   - Place one cake layer on a serving plate or cake stand. Spread a generous layer of maple buttercream over the top.
   - Place the second cake layer on top, pressing down lightly.
   - Frost the top and sides of the cake with the remaining maple buttercream.
   - Pour the pecan caramel sauce over the top of the cake, letting it drip down the sides.

5. **Serve and Enjoy:**
   - Allow the cake to set for about 30 minutes before slicing.
   - Enjoy your Quebec Maple Pecan Cake with friends and family!

This cake combines the rich flavors of maple syrup and pecans, creating a delicious and decadent dessert that reflects the culinary heritage of Quebec.

Alberta Honey Cake

Ingredients:

- **For the Cake:**
    - 2 1/2 cups all-purpose flour
    - 1 1/2 tsp baking powder
    - 1/2 tsp baking soda
    - 1/2 tsp salt
    - 1 tsp ground cinnamon
    - 1/2 tsp ground ginger
    - 1/4 tsp ground nutmeg
    - 1/2 cup unsalted butter, room temperature
    - 1 cup granulated sugar
    - 1/2 cup brown sugar, packed
    - 3 large eggs, room temperature
    - 1 tsp vanilla extract
    - 1 cup honey
    - 1/2 cup buttermilk, room temperature
    - 1/2 cup hot coffee
- **For the Honey Buttercream Frosting:**
    - 1 cup unsalted butter, room temperature
    - 3 1/2 cups powdered sugar
    - 1/4 cup honey
    - 1-2 tbsp heavy cream
    - 1 tsp vanilla extract
    - Pinch of salt
- **For Garnish:**
    - Honey drizzle
    - Candied pecans or walnuts (optional)
    - Edible flowers (optional)

Instructions:

1. **Prepare the Cake:**
    - Preheat your oven to 350°F (175°C). Grease and flour two 9-inch round cake pans.
    - In a medium bowl, whisk together the flour, baking powder, baking soda, salt, cinnamon, ginger, and nutmeg.
    - In a large bowl, beat the butter, granulated sugar, and brown sugar together until light and fluffy, about 3-5 minutes.
    - Add the eggs one at a time, beating well after each addition. Mix in the vanilla extract.
    - Gradually add the honey to the mixture, beating until well combined.
    - Add the flour mixture to the butter mixture in three additions, alternating with the buttermilk, beginning and ending with the flour mixture. Mix until just combined.
    - Stir in the hot coffee until the batter is smooth.
    - Divide the batter evenly between the prepared cake pans and smooth the tops.
    - Bake for 30-35 minutes, or until a toothpick inserted into the center of the cakes comes out clean.

- Let the cakes cool in the pans for 10 minutes, then remove from the pans and transfer to a wire rack to cool completely.

2. **Prepare the Honey Buttercream Frosting:**
    - In a large bowl, beat the butter until creamy and smooth, about 2-3 minutes.
    - Gradually add the powdered sugar, one cup at a time, beating well after each addition.
    - Add the honey, heavy cream, vanilla extract, and salt. Beat on high speed for 3-4 minutes, until the frosting is light and fluffy.
    - If the frosting is too thick, add an additional tablespoon of heavy cream. If it's too thin, add more powdered sugar, one tablespoon at a time, until the desired consistency is reached.
3. **Assemble the Cake:**
    - Place one cake layer on a serving plate or cake stand. Spread a generous layer of honey buttercream frosting over the top.
    - Place the second cake layer on top, pressing down lightly.
    - Frost the top and sides of the cake with the remaining honey buttercream frosting.
4. **Garnish the Cake:**
    - Drizzle additional honey over the top of the cake.
    - Garnish with candied pecans or walnuts and edible flowers, if desired.
5. **Serve and Enjoy:**
    - Allow the cake to set for about 30 minutes before slicing.
    - Enjoy your Alberta Honey Cake with friends and family!

This cake captures the essence of Alberta with its rich honey flavor, complemented by warm spices and a creamy honey buttercream frosting. Perfect for any occasion, it celebrates the sweetness and warmth of this beautiful province.

Saskatchewan Saskatoon Berry Cake

Ingredients:

- **For the Cake:**
    - 2 1/2 cups all-purpose flour
    - 2 tsp baking powder
    - 1/2 tsp baking soda
    - 1/2 tsp salt
    - 1 cup unsalted butter, room temperature
    - 1 1/2 cups granulated sugar
    - 4 large eggs, room temperature
    - 1 tsp vanilla extract
    - 1 cup buttermilk, room temperature
    - 1/2 cup Saskatoon berry puree (see below for instructions)
- **For the Saskatoon Berry Puree:**
    - 2 cups fresh or frozen Saskatoon berries
    - 2 tbsp granulated sugar
    - 1 tbsp lemon juice
- **For the Saskatoon Berry Filling:**
    - 2 cups fresh or frozen Saskatoon berries
    - 1/2 cup granulated sugar
    - 2 tbsp cornstarch
    - 1/4 cup water
    - 1 tbsp lemon juice
- **For the Whipped Cream Frosting:**
    - 2 cups heavy whipping cream
    - 1/2 cup powdered sugar
    - 1 tsp vanilla extract
- **For Garnish:**
    - Fresh Saskatoon berries
    - Edible flowers (optional)

Instructions:

1. **Prepare the Saskatoon Berry Puree:**
    - In a medium saucepan, combine the Saskatoon berries, granulated sugar, and lemon juice.
    - Cook over medium heat until the berries soften and release their juices, about 10 minutes.
    - Remove from heat and let cool slightly, then blend until smooth using a blender or food processor.
    - Strain the puree through a fine mesh sieve to remove seeds. Set aside 1/2 cup for the cake batter.
2. **Prepare the Cake:**
    - Preheat your oven to 350°F (175°C). Grease and flour two 9-inch round cake pans.
    - In a medium bowl, whisk together the flour, baking powder, baking soda, and salt.
    - In a large bowl, beat the butter and granulated sugar together until light and fluffy, about 3-5 minutes.

- Add the eggs one at a time, beating well after each addition. Mix in the vanilla extract.
- Gradually add the flour mixture to the butter mixture, alternating with the buttermilk and Saskatoon berry puree, beginning and ending with the flour mixture. Mix until just combined.
- Divide the batter evenly between the prepared cake pans and smooth the tops.
- Bake for 25-30 minutes, or until a toothpick inserted into the center of the cakes comes out clean.
- Let the cakes cool in the pans for 10 minutes, then remove from the pans and transfer to a wire rack to cool completely.

3. **Prepare the Saskatoon Berry Filling:**
   - In a medium saucepan, combine the Saskatoon berries, granulated sugar, cornstarch, water, and lemon juice.
   - Cook over medium heat, stirring constantly, until the mixture thickens and the berries break down, about 5-7 minutes.
   - Remove from heat and let cool completely.

4. **Prepare the Whipped Cream Frosting:**
   - In a large bowl, beat the heavy whipping cream, powdered sugar, and vanilla extract on high speed until stiff peaks form.

5. **Assemble the Cake:**
   - Place one cake layer on a serving plate or cake stand. Spread a layer of Saskatoon berry filling over the cake layer.
   - Spread a layer of whipped cream frosting over the berry filling.
   - Place the second cake layer on top, pressing down lightly.
   - Frost the top and sides of the cake with the remaining whipped cream frosting.

6. **Garnish the Cake:**
   - Decorate with fresh Saskatoon berries and edible flowers, if desired.

7. **Serve and Enjoy:**
   - Chill the cake in the refrigerator for about 30 minutes before slicing.
   - Enjoy your Saskatchewan Saskatoon Berry Cake with friends and family!

This cake highlights the unique and delicious flavor of Saskatoon berries, combined with a light and fluffy cake and a creamy whipped cream frosting, celebrating the vibrant tastes of Saskatchewan.

PEI Raspberry Cake

Ingredients:

- **For the Cake:**
    - 2 1/2 cups all-purpose flour
    - 2 tsp baking powder
    - 1/2 tsp baking soda
    - 1/2 tsp salt
    - 1 cup unsalted butter, room temperature
    - 1 1/2 cups granulated sugar
    - 4 large eggs, room temperature
    - 1 tsp vanilla extract
    - 1/2 tsp almond extract
    - 1 cup buttermilk, room temperature
    - 1 cup fresh raspberries, lightly mashed
- **For the Raspberry Filling:**
    - 2 cups fresh or frozen raspberries
    - 1/2 cup granulated sugar
    - 2 tbsp cornstarch
    - 1/4 cup water
    - 1 tbsp lemon juice
- **For the Cream Cheese Frosting:**
    - 1 cup unsalted butter, room temperature
    - 8 oz cream cheese, room temperature
    - 4 cups powdered sugar
    - 1/4 cup raspberry puree (see below for instructions)
    - 1 tsp vanilla extract
    - Pinch of salt
- **For Garnish:**
    - Fresh raspberries
    - Edible flowers (optional)

Instructions:

1. **Prepare the Raspberry Puree:**
    - In a medium saucepan, combine 1 cup of fresh or frozen raspberries and 2 tablespoons of granulated sugar.
    - Cook over medium heat until the raspberries break down and release their juices, about 5-7 minutes.
    - Strain the mixture through a fine mesh sieve to remove seeds and set aside 1/4 cup of the puree for the frosting.
2. **Prepare the Cake:**
    - Preheat your oven to 350°F (175°C). Grease and flour two 9-inch round cake pans.
    - In a medium bowl, whisk together the flour, baking powder, baking soda, and salt.
    - In a large bowl, beat the butter and granulated sugar together until light and fluffy, about 3-5 minutes.
    - Add the eggs one at a time, beating well after each addition. Mix in the vanilla and almond extracts.

- Gradually add the flour mixture to the butter mixture, alternating with the buttermilk, beginning and ending with the flour mixture. Mix until just combined.
- Fold in the lightly mashed fresh raspberries.
- Divide the batter evenly between the prepared cake pans and smooth the tops.
- Bake for 25-30 minutes, or until a toothpick inserted into the center of the cakes comes out clean.
- Let the cakes cool in the pans for 10 minutes, then remove from the pans and transfer to a wire rack to cool completely.

3. **Prepare the Raspberry Filling:**
    - In a medium saucepan, combine the raspberries, granulated sugar, cornstarch, water, and lemon juice.
    - Cook over medium heat, stirring constantly, until the mixture thickens and the raspberries break down, about 5-7 minutes.
    - Remove from heat and let cool completely.

4. **Prepare the Cream Cheese Frosting:**
    - In a large bowl, beat the butter and cream cheese together until creamy and smooth, about 2-3 minutes.
    - Gradually add the powdered sugar, one cup at a time, beating well after each addition.
    - Add the raspberry puree, vanilla extract, and salt. Beat on high speed for 3-4 minutes, until the frosting is light and fluffy.

5. **Assemble the Cake:**
    - Place one cake layer on a serving plate or cake stand. Spread a layer of raspberry filling over the cake layer.
    - Place the second cake layer on top, pressing down lightly.
    - Frost the top and sides of the cake with the cream cheese frosting.

6. **Garnish the Cake:**
    - Decorate with fresh raspberries and edible flowers, if desired.

7. **Serve and Enjoy:**
    - Chill the cake in the refrigerator for about 30 minutes before slicing.
    - Enjoy your PEI Raspberry Cake with friends and family!

This cake features the bright and tangy flavor of fresh raspberries, combined with a moist and tender cake and a rich cream cheese frosting, celebrating the bountiful raspberry harvest of Prince Edward Island.

Montreal Smoked Meat Cake

Ingredients:

- **For the Cake:**
    - 2 1/2 cups all-purpose flour
    - 2 tsp baking powder
    - 1/2 tsp baking soda
    - 1/2 tsp salt
    - 1 cup unsalted butter, room temperature
    - 1 1/2 cups granulated sugar
    - 4 large eggs, room temperature
    - 1 tsp vanilla extract
    - 1 cup buttermilk, room temperature
- **For the Savory Filling:**
    - 2 cups Montreal smoked meat, finely chopped
    - 1 cup cream cheese, room temperature
    - 1/2 cup sour cream
    - 2 tbsp Dijon mustard
    - 1/4 cup finely chopped green onions
    - Salt and pepper to taste
- **For the Cream Cheese Frosting:**
    - 1 cup unsalted butter, room temperature
    - 8 oz cream cheese, room temperature
    - 4 cups powdered sugar
    - 1 tsp vanilla extract
    - Pinch of salt
- **For Garnish:**
    - Finely chopped Montreal smoked meat
    - Chopped green onions
    - Fresh dill or parsley (optional)

Instructions:

1. **Prepare the Cake:**
    - Preheat your oven to 350°F (175°C). Grease and flour two 9-inch round cake pans.
    - In a medium bowl, whisk together the flour, baking powder, baking soda, and salt.
    - In a large bowl, beat the butter and granulated sugar together until light and fluffy, about 3-5 minutes.
    - Add the eggs one at a time, beating well after each addition. Mix in the vanilla extract.
    - Gradually add the flour mixture to the butter mixture, alternating with the buttermilk, beginning and ending with the flour mixture. Mix until just combined.
    - Divide the batter evenly between the prepared cake pans and smooth the tops.
    - Bake for 25-30 minutes, or until a toothpick inserted into the center of the cakes comes out clean.
    - Let the cakes cool in the pans for 10 minutes, then remove from the pans and transfer to a wire rack to cool completely.
2. **Prepare the Savory Filling:**

- In a medium bowl, combine the finely chopped Montreal smoked meat, cream cheese, sour cream, Dijon mustard, and green onions. Mix until well combined.
- Season with salt and pepper to taste.
3. **Prepare the Cream Cheese Frosting:**
    - In a large bowl, beat the butter and cream cheese together until creamy and smooth, about 2-3 minutes.
    - Gradually add the powdered sugar, one cup at a time, beating well after each addition.
    - Add the vanilla extract and salt. Beat on high speed for 3-4 minutes, until the frosting is light and fluffy.
4. **Assemble the Cake:**
    - Place one cake layer on a serving plate or cake stand. Spread a layer of the savory filling over the cake layer.
    - Place the second cake layer on top, pressing down lightly.
    - Frost the top and sides of the cake with the cream cheese frosting.
5. **Garnish the Cake:**
    - Sprinkle finely chopped Montreal smoked meat and chopped green onions on top of the cake.
    - Garnish with fresh dill or parsley, if desired.
6. **Serve and Enjoy:**
    - Chill the cake in the refrigerator for about 30 minutes before slicing.
    - Enjoy your Montreal Smoked Meat Cake as a unique and savory treat!

This cake combines the rich flavors of Montreal smoked meat with a savory filling and a creamy frosting, creating a unique and delightful culinary experience that pays homage to Montreal's iconic smoked meat sandwiches.

Toronto Butter Tart Cake

Ingredients:

- **For the Cake:**
    - 2 1/2 cups all-purpose flour
    - 2 tsp baking powder
    - 1/2 tsp baking soda
    - 1/2 tsp salt
    - 1 cup unsalted butter, room temperature
    - 1 1/2 cups granulated sugar
    - 4 large eggs, room temperature
    - 1 tsp vanilla extract
    - 1 cup buttermilk, room temperature
- **For the Butter Tart Filling:**
    - 1 cup packed brown sugar
    - 1/2 cup unsalted butter, melted
    - 1/2 cup corn syrup
    - 2 large eggs
    - 1 tsp vanilla extract
    - 1/4 tsp salt
    - 1/2 cup chopped pecans (optional)
- **For the Maple Buttercream Frosting:**
    - 1 cup unsalted butter, room temperature
    - 4 cups powdered sugar
    - 1/4 cup pure maple syrup
    - 1-2 tbsp heavy cream (if needed)
    - 1 tsp vanilla extract
    - Pinch of salt

Instructions:

1. **Prepare the Cake:**
    - Preheat your oven to 350°F (175°C). Grease and flour two 9-inch round cake pans.
    - In a medium bowl, whisk together the flour, baking powder, baking soda, and salt.
    - In a large bowl, beat the butter and granulated sugar together until light and fluffy, about 3-5 minutes.
    - Add the eggs one at a time, beating well after each addition. Mix in the vanilla extract.
    - Gradually add the flour mixture to the butter mixture, alternating with the buttermilk, beginning and ending with the flour mixture. Mix until just combined.
    - Divide the batter evenly between the prepared cake pans and smooth the tops.
    - Bake for 25-30 minutes, or until a toothpick inserted into the center of the cakes comes out clean.
    - Let the cakes cool in the pans for 10 minutes, then remove from the pans and transfer to a wire rack to cool completely.
2. **Prepare the Butter Tart Filling:**
    - In a medium bowl, whisk together the brown sugar, melted butter, corn syrup, eggs, vanilla extract, and salt until smooth.
    - Stir in the chopped pecans, if using.

3. **Make the Maple Buttercream Frosting:**
    - In a large bowl, beat the butter until creamy and smooth, about 2-3 minutes.
    - Gradually add the powdered sugar, one cup at a time, beating well after each addition.
    - Add the maple syrup, vanilla extract, and salt. Beat on high speed for 3-4 minutes, until the frosting is light and fluffy.
    - If the frosting is too thick, add heavy cream, 1 tablespoon at a time, until desired consistency is reached.
4. **Assemble the Cake:**
    - Place one cake layer on a serving plate or cake stand.
    - Spread a layer of the butter tart filling evenly over the top.
    - Place the second cake layer on top of the filling, pressing down lightly.
    - Frost the top and sides of the cake with the maple buttercream frosting.
5. **Garnish (Optional):**
    - Drizzle additional maple syrup over the top of the cake.
    - Garnish with chopped pecans or a dusting of powdered sugar.
6. **Serve and Enjoy:**
    - Chill the cake in the refrigerator for about 30 minutes before slicing to allow the flavors to meld.
    - Slice and serve your Toronto Butter Tart Cake, savoring the rich flavors of butter tart in cake form!

This cake captures the essence of Toronto's beloved butter tart in a delightful dessert that's perfect for any occasion, combining moist cake layers with a sweet and gooey butter tart filling and a delicious maple buttercream frosting.

Vancouver Coffee Crisp Cake

Ingredients:

- **For the Cake:**
    - 2 1/2 cups all-purpose flour
    - 2 tsp baking powder
    - 1/2 tsp baking soda
    - 1/2 tsp salt
    - 1 cup unsalted butter, room temperature
    - 1 1/2 cups granulated sugar
    - 4 large eggs, room temperature
    - 1 tsp vanilla extract
    - 1 cup buttermilk, room temperature
    - 1/2 cup strong brewed coffee, cooled
- **For the Coffee Crisp Filling:**
    - 2 cups heavy cream
    - 2 tbsp powdered sugar
    - 1 tsp vanilla extract
    - 4 Coffee Crisp chocolate bars, chopped into small pieces
- **For the Chocolate Ganache:**
    - 1 cup heavy cream
    - 8 oz semi-sweet chocolate, finely chopped
- **For Garnish:**
    - Additional Coffee Crisp chocolate bars, chopped

Instructions:

1. **Prepare the Cake:**
    - Preheat your oven to 350°F (175°C). Grease and flour two 9-inch round cake pans.
    - In a medium bowl, whisk together the flour, baking powder, baking soda, and salt.
    - In a large bowl, beat the butter and granulated sugar together until light and fluffy, about 3-5 minutes.
    - Add the eggs one at a time, beating well after each addition. Mix in the vanilla extract.
    - Gradually add the flour mixture to the butter mixture, alternating with the buttermilk and cooled brewed coffee, beginning and ending with the flour mixture. Mix until just combined.
    - Divide the batter evenly between the prepared cake pans and smooth the tops.
    - Bake for 25-30 minutes, or until a toothpick inserted into the center of the cakes comes out clean.
    - Let the cakes cool in the pans for 10 minutes, then remove from the pans and transfer to a wire rack to cool completely.
2. **Prepare the Coffee Crisp Filling:**
    - In a large mixing bowl, whip the heavy cream, powdered sugar, and vanilla extract until stiff peaks form.
    - Gently fold in the chopped Coffee Crisp chocolate bars until evenly distributed. Set aside.
3. **Make the Chocolate Ganache:**
    - Place the finely chopped chocolate in a heatproof bowl.

- In a small saucepan, heat the heavy cream over medium heat until it just begins to simmer.
- Pour the hot cream over the chopped chocolate and let it sit for 1-2 minutes.
- Gently stir the mixture with a spatula until smooth and glossy.

4. **Assemble the Cake:**
   - Place one cake layer on a serving plate or cake stand.
   - Spread an even layer of the Coffee Crisp filling over the cake layer.
   - Place the second cake layer on top of the filling.
   - Pour the chocolate ganache over the top of the cake, allowing it to drip down the sides.
   - Sprinkle additional chopped Coffee Crisp chocolate bars on top for garnish.

5. **Chill and Serve:**
   - Refrigerate the cake for at least 1 hour to allow the ganache to set.
   - Slice and serve your Vancouver Coffee Crisp Cake, enjoying the rich flavors of coffee and chocolate in every bite!

This cake is a delightful homage to the beloved Coffee Crisp chocolate bar, combining moist coffee-infused cake layers with a creamy Coffee Crisp filling and a decadent chocolate ganache topping, creating a dessert that's sure to please any chocolate and coffee lover.

Ottawa Maple Bacon Cake

Ingredients:

- **For the Cake:**
    - 2 1/2 cups all-purpose flour
    - 2 tsp baking powder
    - 1/2 tsp baking soda
    - 1/2 tsp salt
    - 1 cup unsalted butter, room temperature
    - 1 1/2 cups granulated sugar
    - 4 large eggs, room temperature
    - 1 tsp vanilla extract
    - 1 cup buttermilk, room temperature
    - 1/2 cup maple syrup
- **For the Maple Bacon Buttercream Frosting:**
    - 1 cup unsalted butter, room temperature
    - 8 oz cream cheese, room temperature
    - 4 cups powdered sugar
    - 1/4 cup maple syrup
    - 1 tsp vanilla extract
    - Pinch of salt
    - 6-8 slices of crispy cooked bacon, finely chopped (for garnish)

Instructions:

1. **Prepare the Cake:**
    - Preheat your oven to 350°F (175°C). Grease and flour two 9-inch round cake pans.
    - In a medium bowl, whisk together the flour, baking powder, baking soda, and salt.
    - In a large bowl, beat the butter and granulated sugar together until light and fluffy, about 3-5 minutes.
    - Add the eggs one at a time, beating well after each addition. Mix in the vanilla extract.
    - Gradually add the flour mixture to the butter mixture, alternating with the buttermilk and maple syrup, beginning and ending with the flour mixture. Mix until just combined.
    - Divide the batter evenly between the prepared cake pans and smooth the tops.
    - Bake for 25-30 minutes, or until a toothpick inserted into the center of the cakes comes out clean.
    - Let the cakes cool in the pans for 10 minutes, then remove from the pans and transfer to a wire rack to cool completely.
2. **Prepare the Maple Bacon Buttercream Frosting:**
    - In a large bowl, beat the butter and cream cheese together until creamy and smooth, about 2-3 minutes.
    - Gradually add the powdered sugar, one cup at a time, beating well after each addition.
    - Add the maple syrup, vanilla extract, and salt. Beat on high speed for 3-4 minutes, until the frosting is light and fluffy.
3. **Assemble the Cake:**
    - Place one cake layer on a serving plate or cake stand.
    - Spread a layer of the maple bacon buttercream frosting over the top.
    - Place the second cake layer on top of the frosting.

- 4. **Garnish the Cake:**
    - Frost the top and sides of the cake with the remaining maple bacon buttercream frosting.
    - Sprinkle the finely chopped crispy bacon over the top of the cake for garnish.
- 5. **Chill and Serve:**
    - Chill the cake in the refrigerator for about 30 minutes before slicing to allow the flavors to meld.
    - Slice and serve your Ottawa Maple Bacon Cake, savoring the unique combination of maple syrup sweetness and savory bacon!

This cake brings together the flavors of Ottawa's maple syrup heritage with the savory richness of bacon, creating a decadent dessert that's sure to be a hit at any gathering or celebration.

Niagara Peach Melba Cake

Ingredients:

- **For the Cake:**
    - 2 1/2 cups all-purpose flour
    - 2 tsp baking powder
    - 1/2 tsp baking soda
    - 1/2 tsp salt
    - 1 cup unsalted butter, room temperature
    - 1 1/2 cups granulated sugar
    - 4 large eggs, room temperature
    - 1 tsp vanilla extract
    - 1 cup buttermilk, room temperature
- **For the Peach Filling:**
    - 3 cups fresh Niagara peaches, peeled and sliced
    - 1/4 cup granulated sugar
    - 1 tbsp lemon juice
- **For the Raspberry Sauce:**
    - 2 cups fresh or frozen raspberries
    - 1/4 cup granulated sugar
    - 2 tbsp water
    - 1 tbsp lemon juice
- **For the Vanilla Buttercream Frosting:**
    - 1 cup unsalted butter, room temperature
    - 8 cups powdered sugar
    - 1/2 cup whole milk or heavy cream
    - 2 tsp vanilla extract
    - Pinch of salt
- **For Garnish:**
    - Fresh raspberries
    - Fresh peach slices
    - Mint leaves (optional)

Instructions:

1. **Prepare the Cake:**
    - Preheat your oven to 350°F (175°C). Grease and flour two 9-inch round cake pans.
    - In a medium bowl, whisk together the flour, baking powder, baking soda, and salt.
    - In a large bowl, beat the butter and granulated sugar together until light and fluffy, about 3-5 minutes.
    - Add the eggs one at a time, beating well after each addition. Mix in the vanilla extract.
    - Gradually add the flour mixture to the butter mixture, alternating with the buttermilk, beginning and ending with the flour mixture. Mix until just combined.
    - Divide the batter evenly between the prepared cake pans and smooth the tops.
    - Bake for 25-30 minutes, or until a toothpick inserted into the center of the cakes comes out clean.
    - Let the cakes cool in the pans for 10 minutes, then remove from the pans and transfer to a wire rack to cool completely.

2. **Prepare the Peach Filling:**
   - In a medium saucepan, combine the sliced peaches, granulated sugar, and lemon juice.
   - Cook over medium heat, stirring occasionally, until the peaches are softened and the sugar has dissolved, about 10-15 minutes.
   - Remove from heat and let cool completely.
3. **Make the Raspberry Sauce:**
   - In a small saucepan, combine the raspberries, granulated sugar, water, and lemon juice.
   - Cook over medium heat, stirring occasionally, until the raspberries break down and the mixture thickens, about 5-7 minutes.
   - Remove from heat and strain through a fine mesh sieve to remove seeds. Let cool completely.
4. **Prepare the Vanilla Buttercream Frosting:**
   - In a large bowl, beat the butter until creamy and smooth, about 2-3 minutes.
   - Gradually add the powdered sugar, one cup at a time, alternating with the milk or heavy cream, beating well after each addition.
   - Add the vanilla extract and salt. Beat on high speed for 3-4 minutes, until the frosting is light and fluffy.
5. **Assemble the Cake:**
   - Place one cake layer on a serving plate or cake stand.
   - Spread a layer of the vanilla buttercream frosting over the top.
   - Spoon half of the peach filling over the frosting and spread evenly.
   - Place the second cake layer on top of the filling.
   - Frost the top and sides of the cake with the remaining vanilla buttercream frosting.
   - Drizzle the raspberry sauce over the top of the cake.
6. **Garnish the Cake:**
   - Decorate with fresh raspberries, peach slices, and mint leaves, if desired.
7. **Chill and Serve:**
   - Chill the cake in the refrigerator for about 30 minutes to allow the flavors to meld.
   - Slice and serve your Niagara Peach Melba Cake, enjoying the delicious combination of fresh peaches, raspberry sauce, and vanilla buttercream!

This cake captures the essence of Niagara's summer bounty with fresh peaches and raspberries, layered between moist vanilla cake and topped with a creamy vanilla buttercream frosting. It's a perfect dessert to celebrate the flavors of Niagara's renowned Peach Melba dessert.

Manitoba Tiger Tail Cake

Ingredients:

- **For the Cake:**
    - 2 1/2 cups all-purpose flour
    - 2 tsp baking powder
    - 1/2 tsp baking soda
    - 1/2 tsp salt
    - 1 cup unsalted butter, room temperature
    - 1 1/2 cups granulated sugar
    - 4 large eggs, room temperature
    - 1 tsp vanilla extract
    - 1 cup buttermilk, room temperature
    - Orange food coloring (optional)
- **For the Tiger Tail Filling:**
    - 1 cup black licorice candies, finely chopped
    - 1/2 cup sweetened condensed milk
- **For the Vanilla Buttercream Frosting:**
    - 1 cup unsalted butter, room temperature
    - 8 cups powdered sugar
    - 1/2 cup whole milk or heavy cream
    - 2 tsp vanilla extract
    - Pinch of salt

Instructions:

1. **Prepare the Cake:**
    - Preheat your oven to 350°F (175°C). Grease and flour two 9-inch round cake pans.
    - In a medium bowl, whisk together the flour, baking powder, baking soda, and salt.
    - In a large bowl, beat the butter and granulated sugar together until light and fluffy, about 3-5 minutes.
    - Add the eggs one at a time, beating well after each addition. Mix in the vanilla extract.
    - Gradually add the flour mixture to the butter mixture, alternating with the buttermilk, beginning and ending with the flour mixture. Mix until just combined.
    - If desired, add a few drops of orange food coloring to the batter to achieve a light orange color reminiscent of tiger stripes.
    - Divide the batter evenly between the prepared cake pans and smooth the tops.
    - Bake for 25-30 minutes, or until a toothpick inserted into the center of the cakes comes out clean.
    - Let the cakes cool in the pans for 10 minutes, then remove from the pans and transfer to a wire rack to cool completely.
2. **Prepare the Tiger Tail Filling:**
    - In a small saucepan, combine the chopped black licorice candies and sweetened condensed milk.
    - Cook over low heat, stirring constantly, until the candies are melted and the mixture is smooth.
    - Remove from heat and let cool to room temperature.
3. **Make the Vanilla Buttercream Frosting:**

- In a large bowl, beat the butter until creamy and smooth, about 2-3 minutes.
- Gradually add the powdered sugar, one cup at a time, alternating with the milk or heavy cream, beating well after each addition.
- Add the vanilla extract and salt. Beat on high speed for 3-4 minutes, until the frosting is light and fluffy.

4. **Assemble the Cake:**
    - Place one cake layer on a serving plate or cake stand.
    - Spread a layer of the Tiger Tail filling over the top of the cake layer.
    - Place the second cake layer on top of the filling.
    - Frost the top and sides of the cake with the vanilla buttercream frosting.

5. **Decorate (Optional):**
    - If desired, drizzle some additional Tiger Tail filling over the top of the cake for decoration.
    - Use a toothpick to create swirls or patterns to resemble tiger stripes.

6. **Chill and Serve:**
    - Chill the cake in the refrigerator for about 30 minutes to allow the flavors to meld.
    - Slice and serve your Manitoba Tiger Tail Cake, enjoying the unique flavors inspired by the famous Canadian ice cream treat!

This cake combines the sweet and slightly tangy flavor of black licorice with creamy vanilla buttercream and moist cake layers, creating a delightful dessert that pays homage to Manitoba's Tiger Tail ice cream flavor.

Quebec Tourtière Cake

Ingredients:

- **For the Cake:**
    - 2 1/2 cups all-purpose flour
    - 2 tsp baking powder
    - 1/2 tsp baking soda
    - 1/2 tsp salt
    - 1 cup unsalted butter, room temperature
    - 1 1/2 cups granulated sugar
    - 4 large eggs, room temperature
    - 1 tsp vanilla extract
    - 1 cup buttermilk, room temperature
- **For the Filling:**
    - 1 lb ground pork
    - 1/2 lb ground beef
    - 1 small onion, finely chopped
    - 2 cloves garlic, minced
    - 1/2 tsp ground cinnamon
    - 1/4 tsp ground cloves
    - 1/4 tsp ground nutmeg
    - Salt and pepper, to taste
    - 1/4 cup water or beef broth
    - 1/4 cup breadcrumbs
- **For the Potato Topping:**
    - 2 large potatoes, peeled and diced
    - 2 tbsp unsalted butter
    - 1/4 cup milk or cream
    - Salt and pepper, to taste

Instructions:

1. **Prepare the Cake:**
    - Preheat your oven to 350°F (175°C). Grease and flour a 9-inch round cake pan.
    - In a medium bowl, whisk together the flour, baking powder, baking soda, and salt.
    - In a large bowl, beat the butter and granulated sugar together until light and fluffy, about 3-5 minutes.
    - Add the eggs one at a time, beating well after each addition. Mix in the vanilla extract.
    - Gradually add the flour mixture to the butter mixture, alternating with the buttermilk, beginning and ending with the flour mixture. Mix until just combined.
    - Spread half of the cake batter into the prepared cake pan, smoothing the top.
2. **Prepare the Filling:**
    - In a large skillet or frying pan, cook the ground pork and beef over medium heat until browned and cooked through, breaking up any large chunks with a spatula.
    - Add the chopped onion, garlic, ground cinnamon, ground cloves, ground nutmeg, salt, and pepper. Cook for 2-3 minutes, until the onions are softened.
    - Stir in the water or beef broth and breadcrumbs. Cook for another 2-3 minutes, until the mixture thickens slightly.

- Remove from heat and let cool slightly.
3. **Assemble the Cake:**
    - Spread the cooled meat filling evenly over the cake batter in the pan.
    - Carefully spread the remaining cake batter over the meat filling, covering it completely and smoothing the top.
4. **Prepare the Potato Topping:**
    - Place the diced potatoes in a saucepan and cover with water. Bring to a boil over medium-high heat and cook until the potatoes are tender, about 10-12 minutes.
    - Drain the potatoes and return them to the saucepan. Add the butter and mash the potatoes until smooth.
    - Stir in the milk or cream, and season with salt and pepper to taste.
5. **Bake the Cake:**
    - Spread the mashed potato topping evenly over the top of the cake.
    - Bake in the preheated oven for 40-45 minutes, or until the cake is golden brown and a toothpick inserted into the center comes out clean.
6. **Serve and Enjoy:**
    - Let the Quebec Tourtière Cake cool in the pan for 10-15 minutes before slicing.
    - Slice and serve warm, enjoying the savory flavors of the tourtière filling combined with the tender cake layers and creamy potato topping.

This Quebec Tourtière Cake offers a creative way to enjoy the flavors of a traditional meat pie in a unique dessert format, perfect for special occasions or as a savory-sweet treat any time of year.

Alberta Beef Cake

Ingredients:

- **For the Cake:**
    - 2 1/2 cups all-purpose flour
    - 2 tsp baking powder
    - 1/2 tsp baking soda
    - 1/2 tsp salt
    - 1 cup unsalted butter, softened
    - 1 1/2 cups granulated sugar
    - 4 large eggs, room temperature
    - 1 tsp vanilla extract
    - 1 cup buttermilk, room temperature
- **For the Beef Filling:**
    - 1 lb lean ground Alberta beef
    - 1 small onion, finely chopped
    - 2 cloves garlic, minced
    - 1/2 cup diced tomatoes
    - 1/2 cup beef broth
    - 1 tbsp tomato paste
    - 1 tsp dried thyme
    - 1 tsp dried oregano
    - Salt and pepper, to taste
    - 2 tbsp all-purpose flour (for thickening)
- **For the Mashed Potato Topping:**
    - 2 large potatoes, peeled and diced
    - 2 tbsp unsalted butter
    - 1/4 cup milk or cream
    - Salt and pepper, to taste

Instructions:

1. **Prepare the Cake:**
    - Preheat your oven to 350°F (175°C). Grease and flour a 9-inch round cake pan.
    - In a medium bowl, whisk together the flour, baking powder, baking soda, and salt.
    - In a large bowl, beat the butter and granulated sugar together until light and fluffy, about 3-5 minutes.
    - Add the eggs one at a time, beating well after each addition. Mix in the vanilla extract.
    - Gradually add the flour mixture to the butter mixture, alternating with the buttermilk, beginning and ending with the flour mixture. Mix until just combined.
    - Spread half of the cake batter into the prepared cake pan, smoothing the top.
2. **Prepare the Beef Filling:**
    - In a large skillet or frying pan, cook the ground Alberta beef over medium heat until browned and cooked through, breaking up any large chunks with a spatula.
    - Add the chopped onion and minced garlic. Cook for 2-3 minutes, until the onions are softened.
    - Stir in the diced tomatoes, beef broth, tomato paste, dried thyme, dried oregano, salt, and pepper. Simmer for 5-7 minutes, until the sauce thickens slightly.

- Sprinkle the flour over the beef mixture and stir well to combine. Cook for another 2-3 minutes, until the sauce thickens further. Remove from heat and let cool slightly.

3. **Assemble the Cake:**
   - Spread the cooled beef filling evenly over the cake batter in the pan.
   - Carefully spread the remaining cake batter over the beef filling, covering it completely and smoothing the top.

4. **Prepare the Mashed Potato Topping:**
   - Place the diced potatoes in a saucepan and cover with water. Bring to a boil over medium-high heat and cook until the potatoes are tender, about 10-12 minutes.
   - Drain the potatoes and return them to the saucepan. Add the butter and mash the potatoes until smooth.
   - Stir in the milk or cream, and season with salt and pepper to taste.

5. **Bake the Cake:**
   - Spread the mashed potato topping evenly over the top of the cake.
   - Bake in the preheated oven for 40-45 minutes, or until the cake is golden brown and a toothpick inserted into the center comes out clean.

6. **Serve and Enjoy:**
   - Let the Alberta Beef Cake cool in the pan for 10-15 minutes before slicing.
   - Slice and serve warm, enjoying the savory flavors of Alberta beef combined with the tender cake layers and creamy potato topping.

This Alberta Beef Cake offers a savory twist on the traditional concept of cake, blending hearty Alberta beef with creamy mashed potatoes and tender cake layers, creating a unique and satisfying dish that celebrates the flavors of Alberta cuisine.

Saskatchewan Wheat Cake

Ingredients:

- **For the Cake:**
    - 2 cups all-purpose flour
    - 1 cup whole wheat flour
    - 2 tsp baking powder
    - 1 tsp baking soda
    - 1/2 tsp salt
    - 1 cup unsalted butter, softened
    - 1 1/2 cups granulated sugar
    - 4 large eggs, room temperature
    - 1 tsp vanilla extract
    - 1 cup buttermilk, room temperature
- **For the Saskatoon Berry Compote:**
    - 2 cups fresh or frozen Saskatoon berries
    - 1/2 cup granulated sugar
    - 1 tbsp lemon juice
    - 1 tbsp cornstarch mixed with 2 tbsp cold water
- **For the Saskatoon Berry Frosting:**
    - 1/2 cup unsalted butter, softened
    - 8 oz cream cheese, softened
    - 4 cups powdered sugar
    - 1/2 cup Saskatoon berry compote (cooled)
    - 1 tsp vanilla extract
    - Pinch of salt

Instructions:

1. **Prepare the Cake:**
    - Preheat your oven to 350°F (175°C). Grease and flour a 9-inch round cake pan.
    - In a medium bowl, whisk together the all-purpose flour, whole wheat flour, baking powder, baking soda, and salt.
    - In a large bowl, beat the butter and granulated sugar together until light and fluffy, about 3-5 minutes.
    - Add the eggs one at a time, beating well after each addition. Mix in the vanilla extract.
    - Gradually add the flour mixture to the butter mixture, alternating with the buttermilk, beginning and ending with the flour mixture. Mix until just combined.
    - Spread the batter into the prepared cake pan, smoothing the top with a spatula.
    - Bake for 30-35 minutes, or until a toothpick inserted into the center of the cake comes out clean.
    - Remove from the oven and let the cake cool in the pan for 10 minutes, then transfer to a wire rack to cool completely.
2. **Prepare the Saskatoon Berry Compote:**
    - In a medium saucepan, combine the Saskatoon berries, granulated sugar, and lemon juice.
    - Cook over medium heat until the berries soften and release their juices, about 5-7 minutes.

- Stir in the cornstarch mixture and cook, stirring constantly, until the compote thickens, about 1-2 minutes.
- Remove from heat and let cool completely.

3. **Make the Saskatoon Berry Frosting:**
    - In a large bowl, beat the butter and cream cheese together until smooth and creamy.
    - Gradually add the powdered sugar, one cup at a time, beating well after each addition.
    - Add the cooled Saskatoon berry compote, vanilla extract, and salt. Beat until smooth and well combined.

4. **Assemble the Cake:**
    - Once the cake has cooled completely, slice it horizontally into two even layers.
    - Place one cake layer on a serving plate or cake stand.
    - Spread a layer of Saskatoon berry frosting over the top of the cake layer.
    - Place the second cake layer on top and frost the top and sides of the cake with the remaining Saskatoon berry frosting.

5. **Decorate (Optional):**
    - Garnish with fresh Saskatoon berries on top of the cake for an extra touch of Saskatchewan flavor.

6. **Chill and Serve:**
    - Chill the cake in the refrigerator for about 30 minutes to allow the frosting to set.
    - Slice and serve your Saskatchewan Wheat Cake, savoring the combination of wholesome wheat flavors with the sweet and tangy Saskatoon berries.

This Saskatchewan Wheat Cake celebrates the province's agricultural heritage with its hearty wheat base and the delightful addition of Saskatoon berries, offering a delicious and uniquely Canadian dessert experience.

Vancouver Salmon Cake

Ingredients:

- **For the Cake:**
    - 1 lb fresh salmon fillets, skin removed
    - 1 cup breadcrumbs
    - 1/4 cup chopped fresh dill
    - 1/4 cup chopped green onions
    - 1/4 cup grated Parmesan cheese
    - Zest of 1 lemon
    - 1/4 cup mayonnaise
    - 2 large eggs, beaten
    - Salt and pepper, to taste
- **For the Dill Sauce:**
    - 1 cup sour cream
    - 1/4 cup chopped fresh dill
    - 1 tbsp lemon juice
    - Salt and pepper, to taste

Instructions:

1. **Prepare the Salmon:**
    - Preheat your oven to 375°F (190°C). Line a baking sheet with parchment paper.
    - Place the salmon fillets on the prepared baking sheet and season with salt and pepper.
    - Bake for 12-15 minutes, or until the salmon is cooked through and flakes easily with a fork.
    - Remove from the oven and let cool slightly. Flake the salmon into small pieces with a fork.
2. **Make the Cake Batter:**
    - In a large bowl, combine the flaked salmon, breadcrumbs, chopped dill, chopped green onions, grated Parmesan cheese, lemon zest, mayonnaise, beaten eggs, salt, and pepper.
    - Mix until well combined and the mixture holds together when pressed.
3. **Form and Bake the Cakes:**
    - Preheat your oven to 350°F (175°C). Grease a baking sheet or line with parchment paper.
    - Shape the salmon mixture into 8-10 patties, depending on the desired size.
    - Place the patties on the prepared baking sheet.
    - Bake for 20-25 minutes, or until the cakes are golden brown and cooked through.
4. **Prepare the Dill Sauce:**
    - In a small bowl, combine the sour cream, chopped fresh dill, lemon juice, salt, and pepper. Stir until well combined.
5. **Serve:**
    - Serve the Vancouver Salmon Cakes warm, topped with the dill sauce.
6. **Optional Garnish:**
    - Garnish with additional chopped dill or lemon wedges for extra freshness.

Enjoy these Vancouver Salmon Cakes as a delicious appetizer or main dish, celebrating the flavors of fresh salmon in a unique and savory-sweet cake format inspired by Vancouver's culinary delights.

Calgary Beef-on-Bun Cake

Ingredients:

- **For the Cake:**
    - 2 1/2 cups all-purpose flour
    - 2 tsp baking powder
    - 1/2 tsp baking soda
    - 1/2 tsp salt
    - 1 cup unsalted butter, softened
    - 1 1/2 cups granulated sugar
    - 4 large eggs, room temperature
    - 1 tsp vanilla extract
    - 1 cup buttermilk, room temperature
- **For the Beef Filling:**
    - 1 lb lean ground beef
    - 1 small onion, finely chopped
    - 2 cloves garlic, minced
    - 1/2 cup ketchup
    - 1/4 cup barbecue sauce
    - 1 tbsp Worcestershire sauce
    - 1 tbsp brown sugar
    - Salt and pepper, to taste
- **For the Cheddar Cheese Frosting:**
    - 1/2 cup unsalted butter, softened
    - 8 oz cream cheese, softened
    - 4 cups powdered sugar
    - 1 cup shredded cheddar cheese
    - 1 tsp garlic powder
    - Salt and pepper, to taste

Instructions:

1. **Prepare the Cake:**
    - Preheat your oven to 350°F (175°C). Grease and flour a 9-inch round cake pan.
    - In a medium bowl, whisk together the flour, baking powder, baking soda, and salt.
    - In a large bowl, beat the butter and granulated sugar together until light and fluffy, about 3-5 minutes.
    - Add the eggs one at a time, beating well after each addition. Mix in the vanilla extract.
    - Gradually add the flour mixture to the butter mixture, alternating with the buttermilk, beginning and ending with the flour mixture. Mix until just combined.
    - Spread the batter into the prepared cake pan, smoothing the top with a spatula.
    - Bake for 30-35 minutes, or until a toothpick inserted into the center of the cake comes out clean.
    - Remove from the oven and let the cake cool in the pan for 10 minutes, then transfer to a wire rack to cool completely.
2. **Prepare the Beef Filling:**
    - In a large skillet or frying pan, cook the ground beef over medium heat until browned and cooked through, breaking up any large chunks with a spatula.

- Add the chopped onion and minced garlic. Cook for 2-3 minutes, until the onions are softened.
- Stir in the ketchup, barbecue sauce, Worcestershire sauce, brown sugar, salt, and pepper. Simmer for 5-7 minutes, stirring occasionally, until the sauce thickens and flavors meld. Remove from heat and let cool slightly.

3. **Make the Cheddar Cheese Frosting:**
   - In a large bowl, beat the butter and cream cheese together until smooth and creamy.
   - Gradually add the powdered sugar, one cup at a time, beating well after each addition.
   - Stir in the shredded cheddar cheese, garlic powder, salt, and pepper until well combined and smooth.

4. **Assemble the Cake:**
   - Once the cake has cooled completely, slice it horizontally into two even layers.
   - Place one cake layer on a serving plate or cake stand.
   - Spread a layer of the cooled beef filling over the top of the cake layer.
   - Place the second cake layer on top and frost the top and sides of the cake with the cheddar cheese frosting.

5. **Decorate (Optional):**
   - Garnish the top of the cake with additional shredded cheddar cheese or chopped green onions for a festive touch.

6. **Chill and Serve:**
   - Chill the Calgary Beef-on-Bun Cake in the refrigerator for about 30 minutes to allow the frosting to set.
   - Slice and serve the cake, enjoying the savory-sweet flavors inspired by Calgary's famous Beef-on-Bun dish.

This Calgary Beef-on-Bun Cake offers a unique twist on a classic Calgary Stampede favorite, blending tender cake layers with savory beef filling and creamy cheddar cheese frosting, creating a delicious and memorable dish for any occasion.

Ontario Garlic Cake

Ingredients:

- **For the Cake:**
    - 2 1/2 cups all-purpose flour
    - 2 tsp baking powder
    - 1/2 tsp baking soda
    - 1/2 tsp salt
    - 1 cup unsalted butter, softened
    - 1 1/2 cups granulated sugar
    - 4 large eggs, room temperature
    - 1 tsp vanilla extract
    - 1 cup buttermilk, room temperature
    - 4 cloves garlic, minced
- **For the Garlic Cream Cheese Frosting:**
    - 1/2 cup unsalted butter, softened
    - 8 oz cream cheese, softened
    - 4 cups powdered sugar
    - 4 cloves garlic, minced (adjust to taste)
    - 1 tsp garlic powder (optional, for extra flavor)
    - Salt and pepper, to taste

Instructions:

1. **Prepare the Cake:**
    - Preheat your oven to 350°F (175°C). Grease and flour a 9-inch round cake pan.
    - In a medium bowl, whisk together the flour, baking powder, baking soda, and salt.
    - In a large bowl, beat the butter and granulated sugar together until light and fluffy, about 3-5 minutes.
    - Add the eggs one at a time, beating well after each addition. Mix in the vanilla extract.
    - Gradually add the flour mixture to the butter mixture, alternating with the buttermilk, beginning and ending with the flour mixture. Mix until just combined.
    - Fold in the minced garlic until evenly distributed throughout the batter.
    - Spread the batter into the prepared cake pan, smoothing the top with a spatula.
    - Bake for 30-35 minutes, or until a toothpick inserted into the center of the cake comes out clean.
    - Remove from the oven and let the cake cool in the pan for 10 minutes, then transfer to a wire rack to cool completely.
2. **Prepare the Garlic Cream Cheese Frosting:**
    - In a large bowl, beat the butter and cream cheese together until smooth and creamy.
    - Gradually add the powdered sugar, one cup at a time, beating well after each addition.
    - Stir in the minced garlic, garlic powder (if using), salt, and pepper until well combined and smooth. Adjust the amount of garlic to your taste preference.
3. **Frost the Cake:**
    - Once the cake has cooled completely, frost the top and sides with the garlic cream cheese frosting.
    - Smooth the frosting with a spatula or knife for an even finish.
4. **Garnish (Optional):**

- Garnish the top of the cake with additional minced garlic or fresh herbs like parsley or chives for decoration.

5. **Chill and Serve:**
    - Chill the Ontario Garlic Cake in the refrigerator for about 30 minutes to allow the frosting to set.
    - Slice and serve the cake, savoring the savory-sweet flavors of garlic in a unique dessert form.

This Ontario Garlic Cake offers a bold and flavorful twist on traditional sweet cakes, celebrating the culinary versatility of garlic with every delicious bite. Enjoy it as a conversation starter or a unique addition to any meal.

British Columbia Smoked Salmon Cake

Ingredients:

- **For the Cake:**
    - 1 cup all-purpose flour
    - 1 cup cornmeal
    - 2 tsp baking powder
    - 1/2 tsp baking soda
    - 1/2 tsp salt
    - 1/2 cup unsalted butter, melted and cooled
    - 1 cup buttermilk, room temperature
    - 2 large eggs, room temperature
    - 1 cup shredded cheddar cheese
    - 1 cup chopped smoked salmon
    - 1/4 cup chopped fresh dill (optional)
- **For the Dill Cream Cheese Frosting:**
    - 1/2 cup unsalted butter, softened
    - 8 oz cream cheese, softened
    - 4 cups powdered sugar
    - 2 tbsp chopped fresh dill
    - 1 tbsp lemon juice
    - Salt and pepper, to taste

Instructions:

1. **Prepare the Cake:**
    - Preheat your oven to 350°F (175°C). Grease and flour a 9-inch round cake pan.
    - In a medium bowl, whisk together the flour, cornmeal, baking powder, baking soda, and salt.
    - In a large bowl, whisk together the melted butter, buttermilk, and eggs until well combined.
    - Gradually add the dry ingredients to the wet ingredients, stirring until just combined.
    - Fold in the shredded cheddar cheese, chopped smoked salmon, and chopped fresh dill (if using), until evenly distributed throughout the batter.
    - Spread the batter into the prepared cake pan, smoothing the top with a spatula.
    - Bake for 30-35 minutes, or until a toothpick inserted into the center of the cake comes out clean.
    - Remove from the oven and let the cake cool in the pan for 10 minutes, then transfer to a wire rack to cool completely.
2. **Prepare the Dill Cream Cheese Frosting:**
    - In a large bowl, beat the softened butter and cream cheese together until smooth and creamy.
    - Gradually add the powdered sugar, one cup at a time, beating well after each addition.
    - Stir in the chopped fresh dill, lemon juice, salt, and pepper until well combined and smooth.
3. **Frost the Cake:**
    - Once the cake has cooled completely, frost the top and sides with the dill cream cheese frosting.

- Smooth the frosting with a spatula or knife for an even finish.
4. **Garnish (Optional):**
    - Garnish the top of the cake with additional smoked salmon strips, fresh dill sprigs, or lemon slices for decoration.
5. **Chill and Serve:**
    - Chill the British Columbia Smoked Salmon Cake in the refrigerator for about 30 minutes to allow the frosting to set.
    - Slice and serve the cake, savoring the savory-sweet flavors of smoked salmon combined with creamy dill cream cheese frosting.

This British Columbia Smoked Salmon Cake offers a unique twist on traditional sweet cakes, celebrating the coastal flavors of smoked salmon in a memorable and delicious dessert. Enjoy it as a centerpiece at gatherings or as a delightful treat for special occasions.

Newfoundland Pea Soup Cake

Ingredients:

- **For the Cake:**
    - 2 cups split green peas
    - 4 cups water
    - 1 cup unsalted butter, softened
    - 1 1/2 cups brown sugar
    - 4 large eggs, room temperature
    - 1 tsp vanilla extract
    - 2 cups all-purpose flour
    - 1 tsp baking powder
    - 1/2 tsp baking soda
    - 1/2 tsp salt
    - 1/2 tsp ground cinnamon
    - 1/4 tsp ground cloves
    - 1/4 tsp ground nutmeg
    - 1/4 tsp ground allspice
    - 1 cup raisins (optional)
- **For the Frosting:**
    - 8 oz cream cheese, softened
    - 1/2 cup unsalted butter, softened
    - 4 cups powdered sugar
    - 1 tsp vanilla extract
    - 1/2 cup cooked and mashed split green peas (from the soup)

Instructions:

1. **Prepare the Split Pea Soup:**
    - In a large saucepan, combine the split green peas and water. Bring to a boil over medium-high heat.
    - Reduce the heat to low, cover, and simmer for 1 hour or until the peas are very soft and mushy.
    - Drain any excess water and mash the peas until smooth. Set aside to cool.
2. **Prepare the Cake:**
    - Preheat your oven to 350°F (175°C). Grease and flour a 9x13-inch baking pan.
    - In a large bowl, cream together the softened butter and brown sugar until light and fluffy.
    - Beat in the eggs one at a time, then stir in the vanilla extract.
    - In a separate bowl, sift together the flour, baking powder, baking soda, salt, cinnamon, cloves, nutmeg, and allspice.
    - Gradually add the dry ingredients to the creamed mixture, alternating with the cooled mashed split green peas, mixing until just combined.
    - Stir in the raisins (if using) until evenly distributed throughout the batter.
    - Pour the batter into the prepared baking pan and spread it evenly with a spatula.
    - Bake for 30-35 minutes, or until a toothpick inserted into the center comes out clean.
    - Remove from the oven and let cool completely on a wire rack.
3. **Prepare the Frosting:**

- In a large bowl, beat together the softened cream cheese and butter until smooth and creamy.
- Gradually add the powdered sugar, one cup at a time, beating well after each addition.
- Stir in the vanilla extract and mashed split green peas until well combined and smooth.

4. **Frost and Serve:**
    - Once the cake has cooled completely, spread the frosting evenly over the top.
    - Cut into squares and serve, enjoying the unique flavors of Newfoundland pea soup transformed into a delicious cake.

This Newfoundland Pea Soup Cake offers a creative twist on traditional cakes, incorporating savory elements in a delightful dessert format. It's perfect for those who enjoy culinary experimentation and the rich flavors of Newfoundland cuisine.

Yukon Sourdough Cake

Ingredients:

- **For the Sourdough Starter:**
    - 1 cup all-purpose flour
    - 1 cup lukewarm water
    - 1/2 cup active sourdough starter (at room temperature)
- **For the Cake:**
    - 1 cup active sourdough starter (stirred down)
    - 1 cup all-purpose flour
    - 1 cup granulated sugar
    - 1/2 cup unsalted butter, melted and cooled
    - 1/2 cup milk
    - 2 large eggs, room temperature
    - 1 tsp vanilla extract
    - 1/2 tsp baking soda
    - 1/2 tsp salt
- **For the Glaze (Optional):**
    - 1 cup powdered sugar
    - 2-3 tbsp milk
    - 1/2 tsp vanilla extract

Instructions:

1. **Prepare the Sourdough Starter:**
    - In a large glass or ceramic bowl, combine the flour, lukewarm water, and active sourdough starter.
    - Mix until well combined, cover loosely with plastic wrap or a clean cloth, and let it sit at room temperature for 6-8 hours or overnight, until bubbly and active.
2. **Make the Cake Batter:**
    - Preheat your oven to 350°F (175°C). Grease and flour a 9x9-inch square baking pan.
    - In a large bowl, combine 1 cup of the active sourdough starter (stirred down after rising), flour, and granulated sugar.
    - Add the melted butter, milk, eggs, vanilla extract, baking soda, and salt. Mix until smooth and well combined.
    - Pour the batter into the prepared baking pan, spreading it evenly with a spatula.
3. **Bake the Cake:**
    - Bake in the preheated oven for 30-35 minutes, or until a toothpick inserted into the center comes out clean.
    - Remove from the oven and let the cake cool in the pan for 10 minutes, then transfer to a wire rack to cool completely.
4. **Prepare the Glaze (Optional):**
    - In a small bowl, whisk together the powdered sugar, milk, and vanilla extract until smooth and well combined.
    - Drizzle the glaze over the cooled cake.
5. **Serve and Enjoy:**
    - Slice the Yukon Sourdough Cake and serve it as a delicious dessert or snack, savoring the unique tangy flavor of sourdough in a sweet cake format.

This Yukon Sourdough Cake recipe celebrates the Yukon's sourdough tradition in a delightful and unexpected way, perfect for those who appreciate the complexity of flavors that sourdough brings to baked goods.